STAR QUILTS

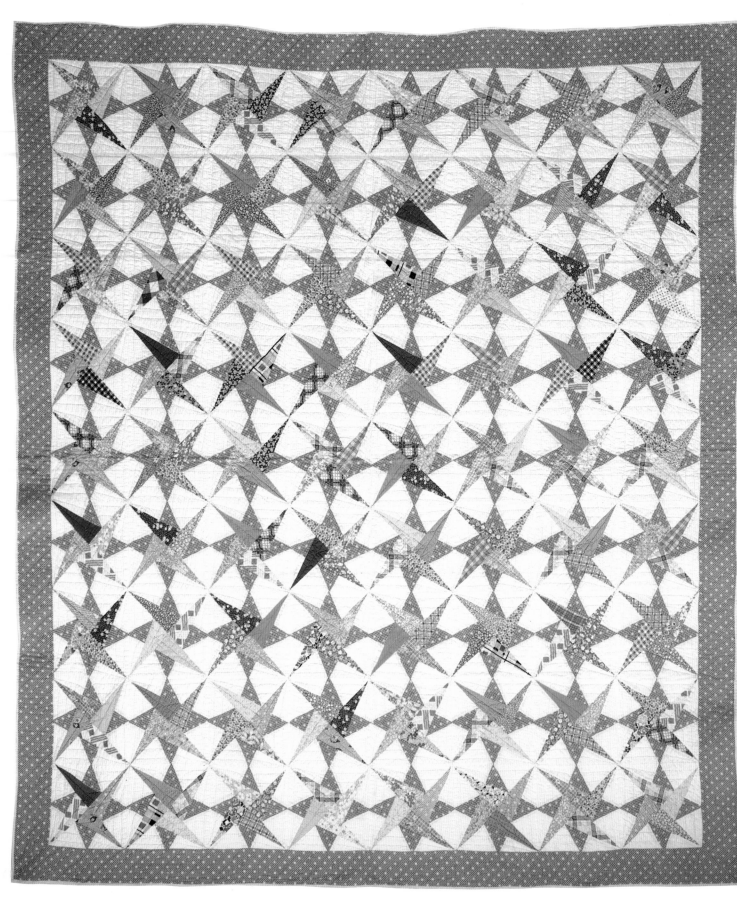

STAR QUILTS

WITH PATTERNS FOR MORE THAN 40 STARS

MARY ELIZABETH JOHNSON

Photography by Mac Jamieson

Additional photography by Ric Moore

Illustrations by Janine Woods

Designed by Alice Cooke

THE QUILT DIGEST PRESS

Simply the Best from NTC Publishing Group

Lincolnwood, Illinois U.S.A.

DL vwm JS RS BV

Photography by Mac Jamieson
Additional photography by Ric Moore
Illustrations by Janine Wood
Designed by Alice Cooke

Library of Congress Cataloging-in-Publication Data
Huff, Mary Elizabeth Johnson
Star quilts : with patterns for more than 40 stars / Mary Elizabeth Johnson
Includes bibliographic references and index.
ISBN: 0-8442-2604-1
1. Star quilts—United States—Themes, motives. I. Title.
NK9112.H78 1997   746.46'041—dc20   96—22658
CIP

COVER — Circular sawtooth settings for Stars of Bethlehem indicate the hand of a master quilter. *Maker unknown; Virginia; c. 1850.*

FRONTISPIECE — A double four-point star is the basis for Starry Paths, a quilt design reminiscent of origami, the ancient Japanese art of paper folding. Clever manipulation of color by the quilter creates rows of pink four-point stars. *Maker unknown; Alabama; c. 1930; 70½ x 80½ inches. Pattern on page 172.*

TITLE PAGE — Detail of a glazed wool calimancoe in the Ohio Star design, which is cross-stitched on the backside of the quilt with the initials "HJS" and the number "4." There are very few examples of numbered quilts. *Attributed to the Jacob family in Groton, Massachusetts; 1771-1825; the red color is from the dye of the madder plant.*

NOTE: The quilts featured in this book are made from all-cotton fabrics and battings unless otherwise stated.

Published by The Quilt Digest Press
a division of NTC/Contemporary Publishing Company
4255 West Touhy Avenue
Lincolnwood (Chicago), Illinois 60646-1975, U.S.A.

6 7 8 9 DN 9 8 7 6 5 4 3 2 1

This book is dedicated to my sister,

Susanne L. Johnson Murray,

who learned to love

and value quilts, as I did,

by watching our mother quilt.

★ ACKNOWLEDGEMENTS ★

Writing a book of this nature is similar to producing a play: when it is finished, it looks so simple. (That is not to say that the author has not made mistakes; it's just that everything appears so pristine and perfect when we can turn pages and see pictures and words.) However, any project like this requires the efforts of many people to come to fruition—it is not a one-woman show, by any means. In this particular instance, there have been literally hundreds of contributors, many of whom I am happy to be able to thank by name, and some of whom are unnamed but have my gratitude nonetheless.

Most important, of course, are the makers of the quilts. I am grateful to those people, many of whom I never met, who accomplished such impressive feats of stitchery. Also, I studied a great many star quilts that are not featured on these pages: there simply was not space for all the quilts (and all the photographs) I garnered in my search. My apologies to those makers and owners of the quilts that do not appear—they were *all* worthy of publication.

I am especially grateful to those independent collectors and to the museums that guard the work of quilters gone before. Robert Cargo of Tuscaloosa, Alabama, deserves special thanks for his generosity in letting me take quilts from his collection to photograph and study, sometimes for months. To Charlotte Hagood, who not only loaned her quilts but has, through the years, encouraged my love of and learning about quilts, I want to express my esteem and gratitude. Andrew Glasgow, with Blue Spiral I Gallery, was an excellent, jovial travelling companion as we combed the country looking for quilt treasures and was most generous with his own quilts. "Miss Margaret" Melzer led us to wonderful quilts, laughing and having a good time while she did so.

I loved working with Gail Andrews Trechsel and Bryding Adams at the quilt sharing days held by the Birmingham Museum of Art throughout Alabama and value their generosity in pointing out wonderful star quilts.

I appreciate the cheerful assistance of Janie Fire and Carla Freidlich of the Museum of American Folk Art in New York. And I owe a debt of gratitude to David Pottinger, whom I don't know personally, but whose collection of Amish quilts I've studied at the Museum of American Folk Art. My thanks also to the staff at the DAR Museum in Washington, D.C., Textile Curator Nancy Tuckhorn, and Registrars Jean Morrisey and Anne Ruth.

Mac Jamieson, the photographer for the bulk of the color work in the book, was a joy to work with and a stalwart partner and support in this project. I am eternally grateful for his attitude as well as his photographs. I am pleased to thank Ric Moore, who helped us finish up the color work and who did the black and white technique photographs. My heartfelt appreciation to Nancy Huihui and Dallas Knight, who demonstrated the techniques as we photographed them.

To all of those people who helped us with locations and props, I wish to express my gratitude: Milton and Kathi Coxwell; Mrs. Paul Hybart; the city of Frisco City, Alabama, and Mayor Ronnie Ray; Susanne Johnson; George and Sherry Blanks; and most especially Curtis Locklin, who was always there when we were desperate for help. John Grant and Charlie and Kathy Grant made the dream of shooting quilts in a cotton field come true; not only did they take time for us while trying to get in their cotton crop, they made us feel that they enjoyed doing it—thank you all! Thank you to Rod Kiracofe, who generously loaned some wonderful photographs.

Janine Woods, who did all the pattern drawings for the book, is a quilter herself, thank goodness. She understood the need to make the diagrams absolutely correct, and to make the pattern pieces fit one another. She took the tissue tracings we had made of quilts and turned them into the accurate patterns you'll find in these pages. And she did it all with a smile, even though the Feathered Stars seemed like a mortal enemy for a time. Thank you, Janine! And thank you, too, to Aileen Woods, who worked with Janine as an illustrator and mechanical artist and happens to be Janine's mother.

One of the great pleasures of my career has been that The Quilt Digest Press has chosen to re-publish this wonderful book. Of the many quilting books I have written or edited, this one is my special favorite. I love it because the quilts themselves practically wrote it—the more star quilts I saw and studied, the more they told me. Also, I love the book because I have such fond memories of working on it with my original editor, Pam Krauss, and the designer, Alice Cooke.

And now my joy in the book continues, thanks to the vision of my new editor, Anne Knudsen, with The Quilt Digest Press. I am most grateful for her faith in the book and her work in steering it through production and marketing channels. My special thanks also to Mark Pattis, John Nolan, Vic Bassi, Gary Facente, and Linda Wolters of NTC/Contemporary Publishing Company for making me feel so welcome.

Finally, and most affectionately, thank you to John Huff, my dear husband, for tending to me so wonderfully and making it possible to finish this project.

CONTENTS

INTRODUCTION

F orget-me-nots of angels …the windows of Heaven…daisies of the sky—stars have had their fair share of heralding by poets, sailors, astrologers. And a worthy subject they are, not only for poets, but for quilters as well.

If stars truly *are* the windows of Heaven, then surely Heaven must be a storehouse of breathtaking star quilts! Ever since Sarah Sedgewick Everett, wife of the governor of the Massachusetts Bay Colony, stitched one of the first quilts in North America in 1704, thousands upon thousands of American quilts have been completed in all manner of shapes, sizes, and patterns, at all economic levels, and for any number of reasons, from economic necessity to the pleasure of artistic expression. But, regardless of their source, intended use, or inspiration, whether born of religious values or marking a blessed occasion such as a marriage or a birth, quilts made in the nearly three centuries since Sarah Everett's have featured star patterns more often than any other. Stars have appeared on American quilts from the very beginning and continue to be the most-utilized design for quilts today. Thousands of quilts contain this motif, either in the "starring" role or in a supporting part.

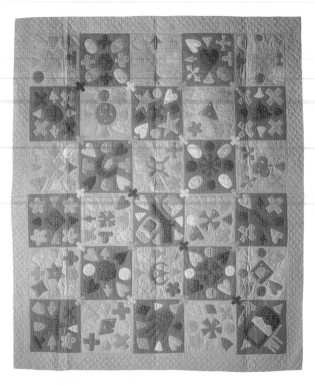

PRECEDING PAGES — Energy fairly
pulsates from a very patriotic quilt;
the red stripes form a pinwheel at the center of
each star. *Provenance unknown; c. 1910;
68½ x 87 inches. Pattern on page 174.*
ABOVE — Popularly called a Cookie Cutter
quilt because of the simplicity of the shapes,
this piece contains familiar motifs from
Pennsylvania German folk art, as well as an
unusual star-and-crescent-moon. *Artist unknown;
probably Pennsylvania; 1875-1900; 71¾ x 80 inches.*
OPPOSITE — An early album quilt
features a variety of star designs. The format is
interesting: a central medallion is
surrounded by rows of unmatched blocks.
*Artist unknown; Philadelphia Pennsylvania;
1842; 92¾ x 96 inches.*

The variety of star designs is quite amazing—
there is a virtual galaxy of them, and there are as many
interpretations of each pattern as there are individual
quilters. Each quilter, of course, takes what is familiar
to her and then adds her own imaginative touches. To

get an idea of the number of different designs (some of
which have more than one name), consider that Barbara Brackman allotted almost one entire volume of
her eight-volume *Encyclopedia of Pieced Quilt Patterns* to
stars. And Yvonne M. Khin, in *The Collector's Dictionary
of Quilt Names and Patterns,* documents at least 160 different stars. Judy Rehmel, in *The Quilt I.D. Book,* by
including all the different ways the same star can be
colored, comes up with an amazing count of 756 star
patterns.

A noteworthy indication of the historical popularity of star patterns is made in the work of Bets Ramsey and Merikay Waldvogel, authors of *The Quilts of
Tennessee.* They studied 1,425 quilts, 7 of which were
made before 1840. Ramsey and Waldvogel found that
almost 12 percent of the quilts they studied contained
stars. They were able to isolate 164 different star
designs; stars were used in the very earliest of the
quilts. The preponderance of stars is significant when
you think of all the other sources of inspiration for
quilt patterns: historical and political events; flowers,
plants, forests, and farms; human and animal forms;
schools, barns, and other buildings; and the endless
abstract geometric permutations possible with the
manipulation of line and color. Some of the most often
repeated designs are quite familiar: Lone Star, Seven
Sisters, Star of LeMoyne, Feathered Star, and Blazing
Star.

It is interesting to speculate about why the star
design is so well loved. Certainly part of the reason has
to do with celestial navigation. Not only were the early
sailors guided across the oceans by the stars in the sky,
they had stars of many points in the compass rose,
which appeared on the sea charts and on the compass
card itself. There is no more wonderful collection of
maritime constellations than in the pieced Nautical
Stars quilt made by Judy Mathieson of Woodland
Hills, California, in 1987. An exploding central star of
twenty points is surrounded by fourteen full stars and
six partial stars, all of different design and of no fewer
than sixteen points. Not only is the quilt of stunning

workmanship and design, it demonstrates the benefits of scrupulous research. The original inspiration came from a nineteenth-century watercolor by an anonymous sailor; further research yielded the compass roses that give dimension to the background. It is easy to imagine the influence that these navigational stars had on women who made the original crossing from the Old World to the New, and on those of later generations who waited for their men to return from their seagoing professions.

Women of the farm were no less
affected by the activity of the heavens. As Rachel and Kenneth Pellman so eloquently put it in their book, *The World of Amish Quilts,* "perhaps this fascination with the

sky stems from the fact that so much of rural life begins and ends at the bidding of the sun. . . . Star patterns, although popular with quilters in general, seem to have been accepted and widely used by the Amish. It suggests a wonderful blending of their respect for God's creation and their love of beauty."[1] Indeed, the names of some of the star patterns suggest the reverence the maker held for nature: Harvest Sun, Starlight, Evening Star, Starry Night, Setting Sun, Shooting Star, Prairie Queen, Starry Heavens, Sunshiny Day, Morning Star, Heavenly Star, and the mysterious Time and Tide. One can imagine the simplicity of a life that allows a quilter to celebrate the goodness of a successful harvest by naming her intricately pieced quilt Harvest Sun.

There are, of course, many references to stars in

A B O V E — Remarkably, each of the twelve blocks of this quilt is worked
in the same pattern; it is strictly the manipulation of color that
gives the impression of so many different stars. *Amish, artist unknown;
Midwestern in origin; c. 1910–1925; 66 x 68 inches.*

the Bible, such as this passage from Job 38:7: "The morning stars sang together, and all the sons of God shouted for joy." What a fine inspiration this verse could be for a devout student of the Bible who was ready to make a quilt! Although the origins of the Star of Bethlehem quilt pattern are not clear, surely it was named for the star that guided the Three Wise Men to the manger where Jesus was born.

Since quiltmakers have always used their craft as a means of expressing political views, it is no coinci-dence that the stars of the United States flag are copied in quilts of a patriotic theme. Indeed, it is some-times the stars alone that make the political statement, as in the well-known pattern that utilizes a star made of eight diamonds, each composed of a red, a white, and a blue stripe. The effect is of bunting, and the stars seem to twirl. The appearance of the pattern seems to coincide with the centennial celebration of this country in 1876 (pages 10 and 11). It appears to be almost impossible to make a political statement in fabric without the use of stars, and it is in these quilts that one has the best opportunity to spot an appliquéd star. It is very difficult to appliqué a star because of the problems of folding under for sharp points and of getting smooth inside corners. Most stars are made by piecing, but, in an attempt to provide visual interest to a plain field, quiltmakers often appliqué stars on patriotic quilts.

The star has always been a part of folk art and has decorated everything from furniture and clothing to barns and buildings. A fine example of this folk art expression is shown in the "cookie cutter" quilt on page 12. There are several different stars on the quilt, one worked with a crescent moon, and they are as integral a part of the design as the hearts and hands we think of as typical of Pennsylvania German motifs. (Interestingly, all are appliquéd stars.)

Not only were stars integral to American folk art, they appear with regularity in designs from all cultures throughout history. Many star patterns can be found in Roman and Arabic mosaic floors and architectural decoration, Renaissance decorative inlay, marquetry on furniture, and the like. Because stars are based on divisions of geometric forms such as squares, rectangles, and diamonds, they have been basic to the repertoire of handcrafters in all media. The smallest pieces of material can be used to make a star design.

This, then, leads us to the practical reasons for the popularity of star designs for quilts. They are infinitely well suited to scrap piecing, in which a scrap bag is emptied out for quilt material. Only the pieces found in the scrap bag are used; the process is the opposite of planning ahead and purchasing specific yardages. And, although stars are not always the easiest of quilt designs to put together, there is virtually no scrap of fabric too small to be worked into a star design.

Another reason for the popularity of star patterns is that they are so versatile. They can be big or small, scattered or organized, in four-, five-, six-, or eight-point designs. The same star can look completely different, depending on whether it is pieced in one, two, three, or four colors. In fact, it is this chameleonlike quality of star patterns that gives rise to the confusion over how they should be named and categorized. Many times, a star pattern has earned an additional name simply because the colors within the star were placed in a way different from the original pattern from which the maker was working. This applies particularly to the Star of Bethlehem, which is also known as Virginia Star, Blazing Star, Texas Star, Kentucky's Twinkling Star, Star of the Bluegrass, Rising Star, Patriotic Star, Morning Star, Evening Star, Stars Upon Stars, Ship's Wheel, Harvest Sun, Prairie Star, Stars of Alabama, Star Bouquet, Star of Hope, Sunburst Star, Glitter Star, Rainbow Star, and Starry Heavens, depending on whom you're talking to. (This is only a partial listing—there are other names for this wonderfully colorful and versatile pattern.)

For an excellent example of the effect of color on design, see the Blazing Star quilt on page 14. What appears to be a sampler of star patterns is really a quilt in which the same pattern has been used for each block—with a different color arrangement in each. It is completely within the realm of possibility that each of the different configurations of color has a different name!

It has been no easy task to arrange this wonderful assortment of stars into categories. I have studied how each of the stars is put together, and grouped like stars together. When possible, I have included a history of the patterns, along with comments on what makes this particular group unique. All the patterns for the stars are grouped together in the back of the book; it is helpful to study them and the piecing diagrams for a clear understanding of how a star is constructed. Construction methods are given in "Techniques and Patterns for Making Stars": included are techniques specific to stars, although they will very likely prove useful in the making of other designs as well. It is very helpful to read the instructional copy;

you will benefit immensely from it even if you don't go straight to work after reading it. That information will be stored away for when you *are* ready to go to work, and it will help you make better decisions regarding fabric and pattern choices.

There is always a source of inspiration for every book, and a fabulous star medallion quilt provided the impetus for this celebration of star quilts. Made in the first quarter of the nineteenth century in either Marion or Selma, Alabama, the quilt combines the influences of the central medallion style, favored by the early English and French settlers, with mosaic pieced work. It features an appliquéd eight-point star embellished with fleurs-de-lis at each tip and set into a larger, pieced eight-point star, which in turn is surrounded by full and partial Stars of LeMoyne. A narrow border of what appears to be twisted rope occurs from the careful cutting of a fabric patterned in feathers. The central medallion is set on point, so that the corners could be filled in with "clamshells" to make a square. The white clamshells are embellished with raised work in floral motifs. A border of half stars follows, and the quilt is finished with a double border of slender diamonds in groups of three blue and three brown alternating around the entire perimeter of the quilt. The final touch is the binding, which is pieced so that each group of brown triangles is bound in blue and each group of blue is bound in brown. The quilt is an exceptionally fine example of the work done in the South before and during the Civil War; later examples similar in style were used as fund-raisers for the Confederate cause.

The oral history that accompanies the quilt makes it all the more interesting. It was made by a Miss Jones, whose father owned a cotton plantation in or near Marion in the early years of the nineteenth century. Some mysterious occurrence caused the father to move the family to Selma, about thirty miles to the southeast. Although the exact reasons for the move have been obscured by time (if indeed they were ever public), it is known that the family intended never

OPPOSITE AND ABOVE — This fabulous pre–Civil War quilt was the inspiration for this book. The original design betrays the French ancestry of the maker with the fleurs-de-lis and the LeMoyne stars. *Made by a Miss Jones in either Marion or Selma, Alabama; 1810-1825; all cotton, some chintzes, never washed; 82¹/₂ x 94 inches.*

to return to Marion: they disinterred their ancestors and reburied them in Selma. Mr. Jones was in the cotton brokerage business in Selma; as hard times became a fact of life after the Civil War, his two daughters began to contribute to the family income. One daughter taught music; the other, the maker of this quilt, taught needlework.

Although it seems logical to assume that this exquisitely worked quilt could have been a teaching piece for Miss Jones when she began taking in students, it was actually made some forty or so years earlier. The Jones family was of French ancestry, which explains why Miss Jones chose the fleurs-de-lis and LeMoyne stars.

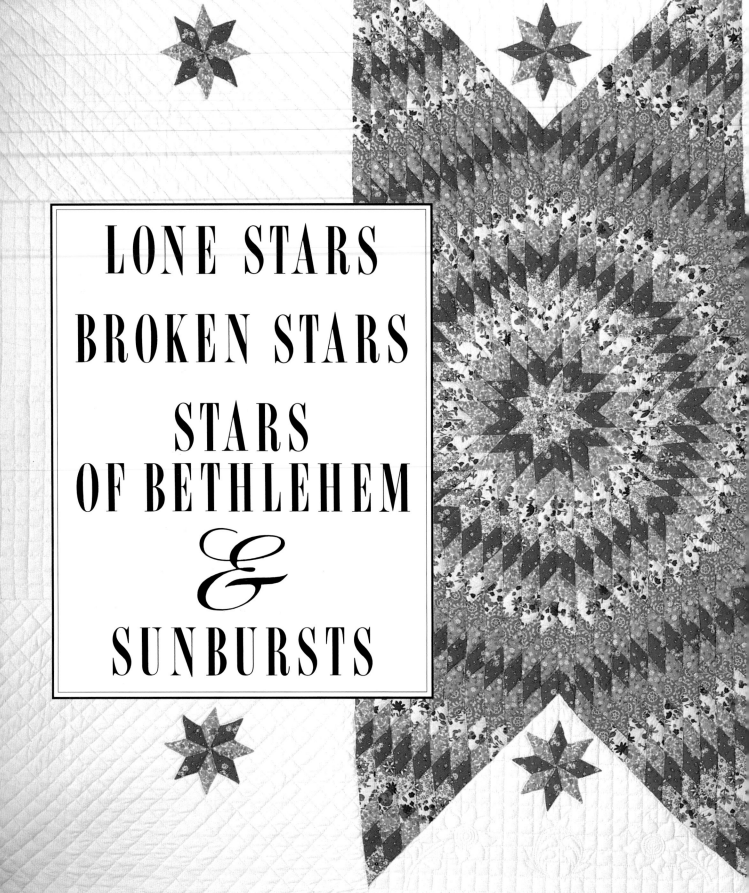

LONE STARS
BROKEN STARS
STARS
OF BETHLEHEM
&
SUNBURSTS

1

When people think of star

quilts, the stars from this grouping are most often the first ones to come to mind. These are the most recognized, and maybe even the best loved, of all the stars. As Gail Binney writes in *Homage to Amanda*, "It would be difficult to choose another pieced pattern that typifies the Americanization of quiltmaking more than Star of Bethlehem."[2]

The classification of patterns within this particular grouping can be somewhat confusing. All of the stars within this group are made from a single diamond that is repeated until a star of the desired size is reached. In one system of naming, the *size* of the star determines the name of the quilt. If one big star has been made, of a size to cover the entire quilt, it has most often been called a Lone Star. The Star of Bethlehem is a smaller star, repeated on the quilt top as many times as the maker

wishes — there are examples that have as few as fourstars and others as many as seventy-two. Strictly speaking, the Lone Star is also a Star of Bethlehem — it was used only once, as big as possible, on the quilt top. Barbara Brackman, who is acknowledged as an expert on the naming and dating of quilt patterns, believes that the name Lone Star actually refers to Texas; according to her research, the big star pattern and the

Republic of Texas were born about the same time. The oldest dated Lone Star has "1835" inscribed on it; that was a year before the fall of the Alamo. There are Lone Stars that are earlier, probably about 1830, but this is the earliest dated example.[3]

The compellingly named Broken Star is a spectacular adaptation of the Lone Star. The tip of each of the eight points of a central Lone Star bursts into three more pieced diamonds, each the size of one of the eight segments of the central Lone Star, and these additional diamonds are arranged to form an irregular circular border. The border requires enough additional piecing of diamonds to make the equivalent of three more Lone Stars! It goes without saying that this pattern is for one who has mastered the technique of piecing those diamonds perfectly.

The Sunburst is related to the Star of Bethlehem, in that it is made of diamonds; it does not, however, maintain a star shape. The spaces between the points of the stars are completely filled in with diamonds; the result is a hexagonal shape filled with rings of colorful diamonds. Another name for it is Starburst.

All of these designs require a great deal of care during hand piecing, because just one mistake in the early stages of construction can cause the star to pucker. Unfortunately, the flaw does not appear until the last diamond is fitted into place, and at that point no amount of pressing or pulling can fix it. Traditionally, these patterns have been respected as one of the real challenges of quiltmaking — out of reach of the novice quilter. They were often chosen for a very special quilt, because they required great skill. In order to achieve a successful Star of Bethlehem or any of the variations, the quilter must have perfected her cutting and stitching techniques as well as have developed a keen sense of color harmony. Although newer, faster, and more accurate ways of piecing have been developed that utilize the sewing machine (see "Techniques and Patterns for Making Stars," page 117), working with these new methods has only increased our respect for the traditional, more time-consuming, hand methods.

Individual manipulation of color has frequently generated different names for the same basic star. A Blazing Star is simply a Star of Bethlehem with the diamonds arranged so that concentric rings of color are formed. A variation of the Blazing Star that is called Prairie Star in *Kentucky Quilts, 1800–1900* carries different names according to the region of the country: it is Harvest Sun in the Midwest, Ship's Wheel in New England, and Star of Bethlehem in Pennsylvania.[4]

Because of the infinite possibilities for interesting color schemes, it is seldom that one finds a Lone Star worked in a two-color scheme; one is shown at right. The Texas Heritage Quilt Society documented a black-and-white Lone Star made as a burial quilt by a Texas frontier mother in the 1860s; she made one for each of her nine children, but one child lived past the time of burying in a pine coffin with a quilt as a shroud, so his quilt survives today.[5] A three-color scheme is also considered rather restrained for a Lone Star.

John Rice Irwin, in *People and Their Quilts*, writes of the superstition, told by a Tennessee mother to her daughter, that a Lone Star quilt would bring bad luck to the person to whom it was given if it had no secondary pattern. The quilter removed the jinx by working smaller stars into the corners of the quilt top.[6] This tale might explain why so many Lone Stars that we see have additional patterns in the open areas of the quilt, but it is more likely that individual quilters just could not resist embellishing a masterpiece.

You will find many examples of the Lone Star, Broken Star, Star of Bethlehem, and Sunburst on the following pages. My intention was to inspire you with color schemes, to show you how a myriad of prints can be combined so that the sum is greater than any one of the parts, and to allow you to compare finishing touches such as corner embellishments and borders. When you are ready to stitch your own quilt, turn to the patterns in the back of the book to find diamonds in many sizes. All the stars in this chapter were made from one of those diamonds, most of them from 2-inch diamonds.

A B O V E — It is rare to find a two-color Lone Star; this is the only one that surfaced in research for this book. The quilting design is outlined in faint, stenciled blue dots, indicating that the quilt was made from a kit. *Provenance unknown; c. 1950; 73³/₄ inches square; 2-inch diamonds.*

A diagram that shows how to construct one point of the star is given there, as is another that shows how the eight points fit together. Be sure to read "Techniques and Patterns for Making Stars" (beginning on page 117), especially those sections that address the Lone Star and the Star of Bethlehem, and you will be able to make *any* of the stars that follow on these pages.

✫ LONE STARS ✫

There is much physical evidence to support the thought that Lone Star quilts were a showcase for a quilter's talents. The three quilts shown here are all about the same age (c. 1850), and they demonstrate the care with which early Lone Stars were stitched. The delicate quilting, their excellent overall condition, and the glaze that remains on the fabrics indicate that all three were "best" quilts, brought out only on special occasions, then carefully put away.

The color choices for the stars and the selection of secondary motifs reveal that the intention of the makers of the quilts below was to produce a masterpiece. We know that the one on the right was a gift to a minister, and surely the maker's best efforts were invoked. In the one on the left, each corner contains an

appliquéd green star, surrounded by four quilted stars that are stuffed with extra cotton. Clearly the maker was proficient in needlework skills, as well as prolific in her application of those skills—this quilt is over 10 feet square, larger than some of today's bedrooms! On the adjoining page, another very large quilt (9⅔ feet square) utilizes many of the same types of chintzes as this first one. A fascinating feature of this quilt is the use of two rows of colored diamonds, separated by single rows of white diamonds. The effect is to emphasize the individual shapes that compose the overall piece. When colors are more subtly integrated, it is easy to overlook the myriad tiny diamonds that make up each of the eight points of the star.

One of the pleasures that await those who make

ABOVE LEFT — Many of the appliquéd chintz cutouts contain Baltimore orioles. *Maker unknown; probably from Maryland or Virginia; 1835–1845; 122 inches square.* *ABOVE RIGHT* — A sawtooth border outlines the points of a Lone Star. *Maker unknown; Perth Amboy, New Jersey; c. 1848; 76¼ x 75⅞ inches.* *OPPOSITE* — This Lone Star is placed on a printed cotton field. *Maker unknown; southeastern Pennsylvania; c. 1830–1850; 116 inches square.*

A B O V E — A trio of quilts airing on a porch railing gives an opportunity to observe three different ways that color can be arranged in the Lone Star. *Provenance of quilt on railing at far left is unknown; c. 1920; 2½-inch diamonds. Quilt at right on railing made by Jeffy Gant; Auburn, Alabama; 1985; 74½ inches square; 2½-inch diamonds.* *A B O V E C E N T E R A N D O P P O S I T E* — The space between the star and the top border on this wonderful quilt allows a tuck-in for pillows. *Made by Julianna Knuettel; Louisville, Kentucky; c. 1950; 75¾ x 91¼ inches; 2-inch diamonds. See pages 138-140 for directions for making all the quilts in this section.*

a star of diamonds is the joy of working with color. There are several ways that color can be arranged. In the majority of Lone Stars, concentric rings of color radiate from the center of the star outward to the points; often, the rings graduate from dark to light to dark again (see quilt on the railing at right). The background on which the star is placed repeats the color of the darkest ring of diamonds.

However, in some quilts the color placement is completely random, perhaps because the maker was using up snippets of fabric: the quilt at the left on the railing is a true scrap star. Surprisingly, this random arrangement of printed fabrics produces a harmonious whole. The quilting emphasizes the geometry of the corner squares and fill-in triangles, and it serves to anchor the star, which otherwise might appear to float in a pink sea.

Certainly the most unusual arrangement of color can be seen in the quilt in the center, in which green spokes radiate from a central hub. The spokes are made of two colorations of the same print. All the fabrics are fascinating; many are classic prints from the 1930s. Some appear to be of the type used in fabric feed sacks. They are skillfully combined; some of the outer rings of color are composed of two different fabrics. Family history has it that the maker saved fabrics for years especially for this quilt, and chose her very favorite pieces for use. Undoubtedly the maker meant for it to be a definitive quilt in her repertoire: not only did she expand the creative potential of a well-known pattern to innovative limits, she used impeccable construction techniques.

The star and border triangles were pieced, then appliquéd to a solid background. (The usual method involves setting in the background with squares at the corners and triangles at the sides.) This magnificent quilt features plumes in opposing pairs between each set of star points, and the background is filled in with rows of quilting in both directions, spaced 1⅛ inches apart, with 8 to 10 hand stitches per inch.

ABOVE — The dark background of this Amish quilt makes the star stand out brilliantly. *Made by Amanda Yoder and her daughter Anna; Honeyville, Indiana; 1930; 75 x 79 inches.* *OPPOSITE ABOVE* — The use of a dark background does not necessarily indicate an Amish quilt; this one is not. *Attributed to Mildred Matilda Buckner; Paris, Missouri; c. 1870.*
OPPOSITE BELOW — This pastel star set on a black background is, however, from an Amish family. *Initialed "M. A. M."; Midwestern; dated December 1921; 70 x 82 inches.*

The choice of a dark or light background can make quite a difference. In most instances, a Lone Star is placed on a white or muslin-colored background, and this is very effective for many color schemes. And, on occasion, a print background has been used to great advantage. However, when a dark background is chosen, the stars seem to glow as in a night sky, as demonstrated by the examples on these two pages. (These three quilts also make liberal but not excessive use of yellow, belying the old notion that "a little bit of yellow goes a long way in a quilt." The dark background and the yellow have an effective, mutually beneficial effect on each other.)

A distinctive feature of the star at the left is the color arrangement—the center of the star is made up of warm colors, up to a ring of black diamonds, where the colors change to cool ones. The use of the warm yellows and peaches in the borders causes the eye to go back and forth between the center of the star and the quilt's edge. Feathered cables are stitched into the wide blue border, and feathered wreaths adorn the corners of the star block.

The quilt at upper right is enhanced by a dia- mond point border and, interestingly, includes colors at the corners that are not seen elsewhere in the quilt. Because the colors are so close in value to the background color, the corners seem to disappear and the symmetry of the light-colored diamonds comes into prominence.

☆ BROKEN STARS ☆

A Broken Star looks like a Lone Star set into a crown. Twenty-four pieced diamonds surround the central star, touching one another and the central star in such a way as to form fascinating undulations of color. Because these twenty-four border diamonds are the same size as the eight in the center star, the maker of the quilt does enough piecing to make three additional Lone Star quilts, giving a certain air of extravagance to the design.

Color is very important to the success of a Broken Star quilt. In most quilts of this type, the pieced diamonds that form the "crown" are done exactly like the eight pieced diamonds that make up the center star. This is the case in both of the quilts below. It is not true for any of the three quilts on the following pages, however. Study each of these quilts to see the differ-ences between the central star and the crown.

It is wise to choose a general color plan before setting forth on a Broken Star quilt. Both of the quilts on this page are worked in mostly secondary colors, but look at the difference between them. The one on the light background is done in pastels except for the small amount of red and the purple. Because the yellows, peaches, and oranges are placed at the outer tips of the diamonds, the points seem to shine. Clear, bright tones of virtually the same colors are used for the quilt on the blue background, but this star seems to be exploding rather than softly shining. A tightly controlled color scheme of a few select hues, such as the one on page 30, makes an understated yet beautiful Broken Star.

The ripples of color in the crown of this design can

OPPOSITE AND ABOVE RIGHT — Subtle gradations of color make a very pleasing quilt. *Provenance unknown; c. 1950; 83¹/₂ inches square.*
ABOVE LEFT — The colors in this Broken Star are reminiscent of a stained-glass window. *Made by Eunice Bush; Milton, Florida; 1987; cotton/polyester fabrics; polyester batting; 84¹/₂ inches square; 2-inch diamonds.*

ABOVE — There is a light mauve in the center star that is not used in
the surrounding crown in this lovely monochromatic Broken Star.
*Maker unknown; designed by Pamela Reising; Indiana; 1986; cotton fabrics,
polyester batting; 85 x 101 inches; 2-inch diamonds.*

A B O V E — The only one of our Broken Stars to be made primarily from print fabrics demonstrates the circular movement that occurs when there is one particularly strong row of diamonds. *Made by Mrs Liverman; Tuscaloosa, Alabama; 1930s; 63 x 75½ inches; 1⅛-inch diamonds.*
R I G H T — The pieced diamonds in the crown of this Broken Star are different from the ones in the star. *Made by Afton Germany; Talledega County, Alabama; c. 1970; 74½ x 76 inches; 2-inch diamonds. See pages 138-140 for directions for making all the quilts in this section.*

create a secondary pattern. An excellent example is seen in the quilt at left, above. The blue fabric makes such a strong secondary design that it is easy to overlook the fact that the big diamonds in the border do not match either the central star or one another. This is truly a scrap quilt, with many wonderful 1930s prints blended together harmoniously. It is a tribute to the maker's skill and planning that she was able to create this completely integrated design with so many different fabrics; most quilters would prefer never to attempt a scrap Broken Star.

Family and friends say that Afton Germany, the maker of the quilt above right, learned quilting from his mother as a child and continued to quilt with her until her death in the mid-1940s. According to Gail Andrews Trechsel and Janet Strain McDonald in *Alabama Quilts,* boys as well as girls between the ages of five and ten routinely learned quilting. Unlike women, men rarely quilted past childhood, when the delineation of male and female roles became more strictly defined.[7] Mr. Germany's Broken Star demonstrates both his meticulous technique and his striking use of color. The addition of the bright yellow-orange to the crown portion of the design is probably the single most important factor in the enormous vitality of this quilt. Two other interesting points are that there are only two prints in the entire quilt (the center star's third row and the star points) and that the diamonds of the crown are not pieced in the same color sequence or even the same fabrics as the center star.

The rings of squares that surround the center star and the corners of Broken Star quilts provide perfect arenas for exquisite quilting. In the quilt on page 30, feathered plumes overlap each other in the borders, and feathered wreaths adorn the squares.

✮ STARS OF BETHLEHEM ✮

A Star of Bethlehem can be made in any size desired, depending on the number of times it is to be repeated on the quilt. It is a good choice for a scrap quilt, because the size of the individual pieces can be quite small, allowing the use of bits of fabric. There do not seem to be many that are actually made of scraps, though. It appears that in most cases the quilts were carefully planned so that each of the stars was the same. This may be a tribute to the complexity of the pattern and the respect with which the quilter approached the piecing of the myriad diamonds.

Although no Star of Bethlehem quilt could be called ordinary, the two on these pages are exceptional examples of the genre. A fine old quilt, below, stands as an exception to the general rule about color planning. Nine stars have been put together with no attempt at uniformity of color scheme. Each of the blocks could have had a different name so far as the maker was concerned; Stars Upon Stars was a favorite name for this design, as was Blazing Star. The smaller stars, or sunbursts, used as a secondary design, seem to float above the rest of the design.

OPPOSITE — Each of these Stars of Bethlehem is done in a different color plan. *Provenance unknown; c. 1840; 107¹/₂ x 112¹/₂ inches.*

ABOVE — Circular sawtooth settings for Stars of Bethlehem indicate the hand of a master quilter. *Maker unknown; Virginia; c. 1830.*

In the instance on page 33, the maker proved that she was no average quilter when she chose to set her Stars of Bethlehem into a circle, rather than the more usual square. She then edged each circle, first with a round of plain fabric, then with a pieced red-and-white sawtooth band. The pieced border and the use of highly prized chintz for the outer border indicate that this was a special quilt to the maker.

The first two Star of Bethlehem quilts each included nine stars; the three following examples contain from twelve to seventy-two stars. In the first example, age has faded the traditional red, white, and blue color scheme of the twelve stars and the narrow, unobtrusive sashing into an easy blending of neutral blues and rusts. The owner remembers her great-grandmother, who made the quilt, discussing the dyeing of fabrics with natural materials such as madder and indigo.

The quilt with seventy-two stars, as well as the one on the following two pages, was made with random scraps. Nonetheless, they were both carefully planned. The one on these pages is put together with pink sashing and white corner blocks. Because the star blocks all have a pink triangle set into each corner, they gain an octagonal appearance. It is evident that the maker saved all the household textiles, including everyone's cast-off clothing, for her quiltmaking, and that she was quite proficient at the art of piecing.

Although the quilt on the following pages is almost square, the red "lightning streaks" are so dominant that our eyes can't help but follow them up and down its length. Hundreds of old fabrics were used for the twenty-five stars, and each is beautifully stitched with tiny 1-inch diamonds.

TOP — Twelve Stars of Bethlehem in shades of indigo and madder have attained the soft patina that comes with age. This quilt now belongs to the great-granddaughter of the maker. *Made by Nancy Nichols Butler; Madison County, Alabama; c. 1870; 2-inch diamonds.*

ABOVE AND OPPOSITE BOTTOM — Seventy-two stars are cheerfully bound together into a whole with pink sashing and white corner blocks. *Made by Mrs. Tenpenny; Cannon or Rutherford County, Tennessee; before 1935; 65 x 75 inches; 1-inch diamonds.*

OPPOSITE AND ABOVE — An exuberant sense of action dominates this old quilt. The red "streak o' lightning" set plays counterpoint to stars that explode with color. The star with the strongest color impact was placed in the center of the quilt. *Provenance unknown; c. 1850; 84 x 86 inches; 1-inch diamonds. See pages 138-140 for directions for making all the quilts in this section.*

✮ SUNBURSTS ✮

Sunburst and sometimes Starburst are the names accorded this overall design of pieced diamonds. An eight-pointed star nestles in the center, and two diamonds are fitted in between each of the eight points to start the sequence for filling in the whole square of the design. At first glance, it looks like a Lone Star with the spaces between the points filled in, but that is not the case—the eight integral units are either triangles or elongated diamonds, not the equilateral diamonds that make the Lone Star. The design can be made large enough to cover the entire quilt top with one giant mosaic, or smaller units can be made and repeated. The difficulty of hand piecing this pattern can be truly appreciated when you count the number of small triangles that must be fitted into the outer edge of the Sunburst to make a smooth-sided octagon.

Concentric rings of color are generally the rule in this magnificent pattern. The coloration of the stunning quilt at right reminds one of agate—the one bright blue round provides the perfect accent to the striations of earth tones in the rest of the quilt. Also, there is one ring of color, composed of three rounds of diamonds, that looks very much like tortoiseshell.

In the quilt above, it appears that the maker attempted to stay with concentric rings of color for all four of her Sunbursts, but had a shortage of fabrics. She was able to match the center square of the quilt to the border. The fabrics of this quilt are fragile, although they are not torn, and the backing fabric and the pale peach used for the background are thought to be hand dyed, possibly with red clay. Even into the twentieth century, the lack of commercial dyes in rural areas necessitated the use of berries and red clay for dyeing.

MUSEUM OF AMERICAN FOLK ART, NEW YORK; GIFT OF C. AND M. O'NEIL.

OPPOSITE — Multiples of the Sunburst designs are
also very effective on a quilt top. *Maker unknown; Tuscaloosa,
County, Alabama; c. 1900; 76 x 78 inches; 2-inch diamonds.*
ABOVE — The technical skill required to complete a piece of
this size and lovely coloration could come only with a combination
of practice and talent. *Made by Rebecca Scattergood Savery,
Philadelphia, Pennsylvania; c. 1840; 118½ x 125⅛ inches. See pages
138-140 for directions for making all the quilts in this section.*

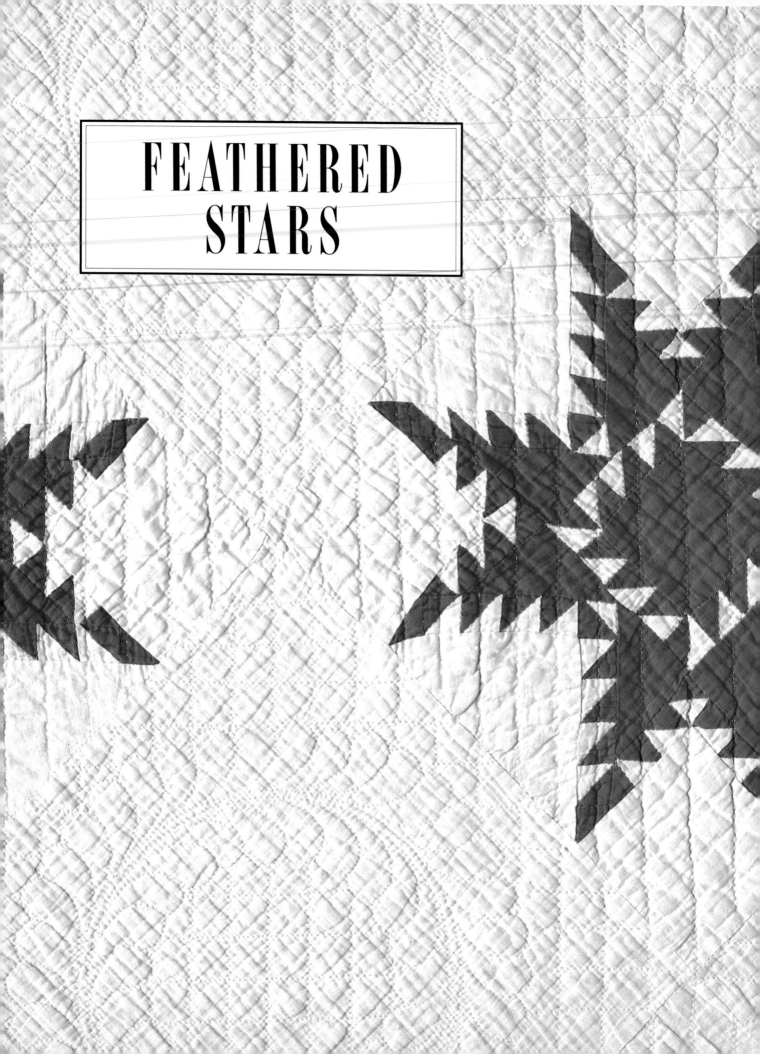

FEATHERED STARS

The grandes dames *of star*

quilts, Feathered Stars are considered by many enthusiasts to be the most breathtaking of all quilts. There is enormous variety within the general grouping of Feathered Stars; however, the distinguishing characteristic of the category is the pieced border of triangles that outlines each point of the star. The centers of the stars can be almost any shape. Squares seem to be the most popular choice, but a square can be embellished with other stars, rows of the same border triangles, or intricate quilted designs. Very often, a center square will be pieced as a nine-patch or a sixteen-patch, or even a twenty-five-patch. Other popular shapes are circles and hexagons.

The Feathered Star was, in the past, considered to be a difficult pattern to piece, and is still regarded with respect by today's quilters. Because of the skill required

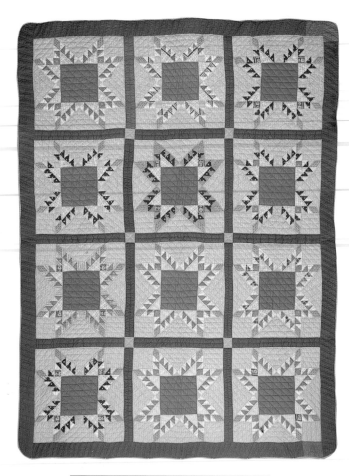

By far the most common star in this category is one with eight points; it is usually simply named Feathered Star, although Sawtooth Star, Twinkling Star, and Radiant Star are names that have been applied. ("Sawtooth Star" has also been used for the Ohio Star and the Variable Star; see "Stars and Squares," pages 48 to 57.) Occasionally the name will be enhanced with a description of the center motif, such as "Feathered Star with Mariner's Compass Center."

The second most common star in this grouping is the four-point; interesting names such as Pine Burr, Pine Cone, and Feathered World Without End have been applied to this distinctive pattern. Occasionally a feathered five-point has been made, but they are rare. There do not seem to be any six-point Feathered Stars.

The traditional method of making the distinctive pieced border of triangles is to cut each triangle separately and stitch them together by hand in pairs of one light, one dark so that little squares are formed; those little squares are then set into strips as required by the design. Innovative and ambitious modern quilters have explored and developed new and faster ways of making this "feathering" strip. We share some of these shortcut methods with you in "Techniques and Patterns for Making Stars," page 117.

There are two types of feathering—open and closed. Some feathered stars appear to have open, or sawtooth, edges; that is because there is a lot of contrast between the light and the dark triangles of the stripping. Most often, the light triangles are of the same fabric as the background of the block into which the star is set. On the stars that appear to have a smooth edge, there is very little contrast between the triangles, and there is also slight contrast between the feathered strip and the background of the star. This phenomenon should be noted carefully by those intending to make this type of quilt; it would be quite a surprise to want that sawtooth effect and miss it because this element was overlooked. In the quilt on these pages, there is one star that has closed edges; it is in the center of the second row.

PRECEDING PAGES — Feathered Stars and feathered wreaths in the quilting make a *piece de résistance. Provenance unknown; c. 1850.*
ABOVE AND OPPOSITE — The most dominant block of this lovely quilt contains triangles of tan, the only solid fabric used other than green and and gold. This quilt has stayed in the family of the maker; it is currently owned by her granddaughter. *Made by Isabella Carolina Harper; Herbert, Alabama (Conecuh County); prior to her marriage in 1881 to James Madison Foshee.*

to piece the star, the prevailing attitude has been that each aspect of the quilt—the center of the star, the open areas of the design, the borders, secondary designs, and the quilting itself—deserves painstaking attention. Perhaps because of the time this kind of attention to detail takes, there do not seem to be as many Feathered Stars as there are other star quilts.

A two-color scheme has been a great favorite for Feathered Star quilts. It allows the intricate piecing to show up clearly. The theory whispered among quilt historians that many quilters made their very best quilts in only two colors is certainly supported by the three on these pages.

Many contemporary quilts are examples of fine craftsmanship, as in the California Star quilt. The center square of each star is a nine-patch block, with five of those patches worked as miniature Ohio Stars. The corner piece of each of the tiny Ohio Stars is also the corner piece for the feathering strip—advance planning was an integral part of this quilt. A concern of the maker was finding a dark blue print that was diminutive enough in scale to retain its integrity in the extremely small pieces of the miniature stars; she wanted a two-color quilt, but she wanted a print for interest. She succeeded in having both. The only embellishment is a beautifully quilted wreath in each of the white squares.

Red and white has been a favorite color scheme of quilters since the beginning of the eighteenth century, when they yearned for the colorfast "Turkey reds" from India. The color scheme is particularly suited to Feathered Star; in this example, the points are lengthened, giving the stars a graceful, elongated aspect. This star is built around a center square that has been embellished with the same feather stripping as the star points. Because the feathers all point in the same direction around the square, a whirling effect is achieved.

In the green-and-white quilt at right, the stars are longer than they are wide (22 x 20 inches). The center square of each is divided into four triangles by narrow stripping in the Flying Geese pattern, which is extremely compatible with the feathering of the stars. Another compatible pattern is the rickrack design of the innermost border. Two dye lots of green fabric were used; the color of the stars remains stable, while the border is changing.

The centers of feathered stars are not always squares or variations thereon. An octagonal center is

OPPOSITE ABOVE — There are one hundred 3-inch stars in this contemporary blue-and-white California Star. *Made by Bettye Kimbrell; Mount Olive, Alabama; 1979; 79½ x 101½ inches.*

OPPOSITE BELOW — Feathered stripping surrounds the center square in a red-and-white Feathered Star. *Provenance unknown; c. 1850.*

ABOVE — This outstanding green-and-white quilt won a prize at a local fair. The field of nine Touching Feathered Stars is almost overshadowed by the fascinating botanical border, which is surely an original design. *Maker unknown; Pennsylvania; c. 1850; 82 x 87 inches.*

A B O V E — The alliance of color scheme, border treatment, and quilting
technique gives this contemporary quilt the look of a treasured antique.
Made by Deborah Bird Timby; Spring Valley, California; 1987; 68 inches square.
Pattern on page 142. *O P P O S I T E* — The most unusual of all our
Feathered Star quilts, this one shows a sixteen-point shape in the center of
each of the big stars. *Made by Rebecca Davis; Five Points, Alabama*
(Chambers County); prior to 1884; 77¹/2 x 68¹/2 inches.

combined with finely feathered points at left to make a variation known as Radiant Star. In this particular example, the time-honored color scheme of red, green, and white has been used. Many older quilts utilize these colors, in part because they were readily available. There were innumerable small green prints available from the early part of the nineteenth century. Many times, a quilter would deliberately mix several different green prints to execute a design. This twentieth-century quilter followed that tradition in her original border design, which is a combination of pomegranates, leaves, and scalloped appliqués, some of which are done in small plaids, others in checks.

The elaborate center of this Feathered Star contains a sixteen-point star or sunflower shape. It is no mean feat to piece a pattern with tiny points, but to set the resulting circle into another fabric, as was done here, takes a sure hand indeed. The stars are large—each block is 24 inches square. The quilt is wider than it is long, which explains the half stars at the top of the quilt, where pillows and a separate pillow cover would be used.

The inexplicable aspect of this otherwise superb quilt is the red-and-white dotted fabric used for the top and bottom borders. It could have been added later, but that does not seem to be the case, as the bands are fitted into the background and quilted as one with the rest of the quilt. Maybe the quilter simply thought the bands would not show when the quilt was on the bed. Her decision was particularly unfortunate because not only is the color visually jarring, it has crocked, or rubbed off, onto other areas of the quilt.

3

The names Ohio Star and

Variable Star are used interchangeably in much of quilt

literature, with the term Variable Star being applied to

the Ohio Star more often than the other way around; if

truth be told, almost every star pattern in existence has

been called Variable Star! The name Variable Star is

purely descriptive; more obscure is the origin of the

name Ohio Star—the design is certainly much older

than the American river or state. Perhaps the name was

adopted for the design as exploration of the continent

progressed. Both designs are called Sawtooth Star in

many old references, which only adds to the confusion,

because that name was used also for Feathered Stars.

The difference between the two designs, in quilt

terminology, is that the Ohio Star is a nine-patch block;

the Variable Star is a sixteen-patch block. Both are

made up of a central square surrounded by eight points;

STARS
&
SQUARES

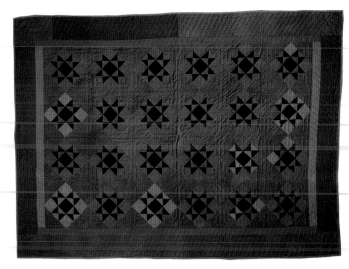

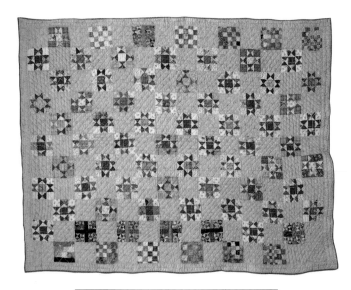

MUSEUM OF AMERICAN FOLK ART, NEW YORK; GIFT OF DAVID POTTINGER.

T O P — The misplacement of color in some of the blocks was probably deliberate. *Amish, maker unknown; Midwestern United States; 1910–1925; 74 x 88 inches.* *A B O V E* — Two block designs besides the Ohio Star can be found in this quilt: Checkerboard (with thirty-six squares in each 5-inch block) and Bowtie (there are sixteen tiny bowties in each block). *Maker unknown; Montgomery County, Alabama; c. 1900; 60¹/₂ x 76¹/₂ inches.* *O P P O S I T E* — Symbols in the quilting represent a young man's favorite activities. *Made by Elisabet Betancourt; Chickasaw, Alabama; 1986; 87 x 104 inches. Pattern on page 145.*

consummate skill; the quilt stands as definition of the ultimate capitalization on a design.

In each of the three quilts on these two pages, a very forthright application of the Ohio Star has been made. In every example, a single star constitutes the patterned block; also, the patterned blocks are set with alternating plain, unpatterned blocks; and in the quilts at upper left and at right, the blocks have been set on point—in the other one, the blocks are lined up in straight rows. It is worth pointing out these similarities because the final appearance of the quilts is very different. No better illustration is needed to show the way that a quilt takes on the personality of the individual who makes it.

In the Amish quilt at upper left, there are such interesting idiosyncrasies in some of the blocks that they can only be deliberate mistakes. The sometimes jarring inconsistencies in otherwise flawless pieces stem from a popular superstition among quilters of varying religious backgrounds that it is bad luck or a sin to make a perfect quilt, since only God is perfect. In meticulously executed quilts, these errors are sometimes so obvious as to become a measure of the quilter's humility. Here, the selection and use of color indicate a skilled artist. With such careful planning, it is unlikely that the flaws in color placement were accidental.

The quilt at lower left apparently was made as a gift. There is an inscription on the back which reads: "To May from Aunt Avver." It is fashioned from hundreds of different fabrics from the late nineteenth century; we may imagine that they were drawn from a personal collection of scraps and snippets, and that the lovely print of stylized leaves on a cream background used for the setting blocks was chosen to make an especially captivating appearance. Perhaps the blocks that are not Ohio Stars were made especially at the request of the esteemed May.

Another gift quilt is on page 53. A mother made it for her son. She chose fabrics reminiscent of men's ties—paisleys, dark prints, foulards, and pindots. The

A B O V E — If there is a quintessential star quilt, "Ohio Star, Ohio Star," has to be it. *Designed and made by Patti Connor; Collinsville, Illinois; 1980; 81 inches square. Pattern and piecing diagrams on pages 146 to 147.*

ABOVE LEFT — A diagonal set to the blocks, combined with an unusual quilting design, gives a sense of movement to Starry Evening. *Made by Patricia Apel; Little Rock, Arkansas; 1985; 53 x 66¹/₂ inches. Pattern on pages 148 to 149.*
ABOVE RIGHT — This quilt is made distinctive by the massing of the star blocks in the center. *Made by Sharyn Craig; San Diego, California; 1984; 52 x 64 inches.*

quilting in the border contains pertinent information, such as her name, the date the quilt was made, the name of the pattern, the schools the son attended, the sports in which he participated, as well as figures of some of his favorite things—there are cars, guitars, fish, and basketballs.

The three quilts on these pages explore unconventional design variations of Ohio Star. The one thing common to these three quilts is that they all employ a unique way of setting the blocks together—not the same way in each case, but a way that is different from

those three we've just seen. In the quilt at left, the patterned blocks are set next to one another so that the secondary design can emerge; in the quilt above left, the stars are sewn into diagonal strips with such spacing that the points look elongated; in the third quilt, at right, the patterned blocks are massed at the middle of the quilt. (In the second and third quilts the contribution made by the borders is important to the success of each design. In each case the borders provide strong visual "fences" to fields of floating stars, leading the eye back into the quilt.)

✷ VARIABLE STARS ✷

The Variable Star has very much the same history as the Ohio Star; it was used in English quilts as a border motif before it was adapted as a block design for American quilts. In fact, there is a variation of the Variable Star that still retains its English name, Northumberland Star. According to Jean DuBois, writing in *A Galaxy of Stars*, each of the triangles in the design is said to represent one of the domains conquered by King Edwin, who lived from A.D. 585 to 633, as he built the monarchy of Northumbria. Edwin eventually conquered all of England except the kingdom of Kent; he then married the king of Kent's sister. Northumberland Star is a Variable Star with a second set of points (necessary perhaps to represent all those conquered fiefdoms). There is another variation of Variable Star known as Rising Star, in which a smaller Variable Star appears within the center square of the large star.

The basic concept of Variable Star is simple, and the Amish quilt below demonstrates how stunning the design can be when it is fully exploited. Stars are set within stars, and stars hold down the corners of the design. The contemporary quilt at right also maximizes the potential of the design by treating it in a very direct manner—with sashing (in a design known as Attic Windows) and a splendid border fabric.

OPPOSITE — The Amish maker blended unusual colors into a
harmonious whole. *Made by a member of the Glick family; Lancaster,
Pennsylvania; c. 1890; wool with cotton backing; 75½ x 81 inches.*
ABOVE — Forty Variable Stars make a sensational quilt.
*Made by Sharyn Craig; San Diego, California; 1988;
60 x 80 inches. Pattern on page 175.*

4

Unbelievable as it sounds,

only one pattern piece is required to make any of the quilts in this category: a diamond. Six diamonds go into each star, and three diamonds make each hexagon. The size of the diamond is the same for both the star and the hexagon, so there is truly just one pattern piece. Placement of color becomes very important to achieve pattern variation. One of the best-known and most-beloved variations of this design is Tumbling Blocks (also known as Baby Blocks), in which the color is arranged so that cubes emerge from the design. In some of these quilts the stars are colored, and in others the hexagons are colored. The size of the diamonds varies broadly; this is a very versatile design.

These quilts are not made from square blocks set together; instead, the stars are pieced together, and then a diamond of the hexagon color is stitched between each

STARS
&
HEXAGONS

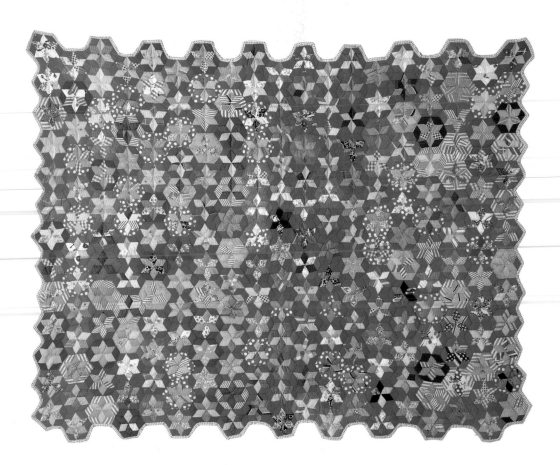

PRECEDING PAGES — Silk stars and velvet hexagons make an
unusual adaptation of this pattern. *Provenance unknown;
found on Nantucket Island, Massachusetts; c. 1880-1900; 51½ inches square.*
ABOVE — This little quilt gets its spirit from the color red.
Provenance unknown, possibly Chambers County, Alabama; c. 1965; 55½ x 72 inches.
OPPOSITE — Big diamonds make big stars and hexagons, and the
effect is dramatic. *Made by Lori Moore; Pensacola, Florida;
1985; 90½ x 86 inches.*

pair of star points. The resulting finished shape is itself a hexagon. Half and quarter diamonds fill in the sides of the quilt where necessary.

It should be noted that the diamonds used to make these quilts are of a different shape than the ones used to make eight-point stars. Two different size six-point diamonds are given on page 151. They are the correct sizes for the pink Stars and Hexagons and for the blue Tumbling Blocks on page 63. If you want to make a large star, such as the one on page 61, you can make your own pattern by following the directions for the Super Star, page 132, with one important difference: the angle of the first point must be 60 degrees

rather than 45 degrees. You will draw a line the length that you want one side of the star to be, then use a protractor to measure 60 degrees from that line and draw in the second line. The second angle of the diamond will, of course, measure 120 degrees. Measure that angle, then draw in the third side of the diamond. Finishing will be easy. It is a good idea to practice drawing this diamond on a smaller scale before you make the large one.

The two quilts on these pages use diamonds that are opposite extremes in size. The one at right uses a diamond with sides that are 8½ inches long, while the one at the top of this page utilizes a 1¼-inch diamond

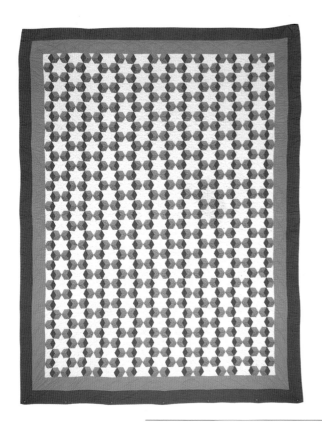

OPPOSITE — Two quilts illustrate the two different ways that color can be placed in this design. The placement of prints and solids in one quilt is the opposite of the other. *Patterns for both on page 151.*

ABOVE LEFT — The dark blue diamonds are arranged so that they form continuous chains up and down the quilt. This ingenious manipulation of color makes a relatively simple design noteworthy. *Provenance unknown; c. 1950; 73³/₄ x 94³/₄ inches.*

ABOVE RIGHT — Two pink prints make up the 95 stars, and white is used for the 171 hexagons. *Pieced by Cassie Rambo; quilted by Mildred Hall; Pensacola, Florida; 1985; 85 x 93 inches.*

(the same size used for the blue Tumbling Blocks). The one with large diamonds is easily put together, but all those large areas must be quilted with care.

In the quilt on page 60, every star has either a solid red, red polka dot, or red-striped background. The stars themselves are all kinds of fabrics—many colors, prints, and solids. Little red hexagons appear when stars with a solid background are set together, and Tumbling Blocks are formed when three different fabric join one another. The Tumbling Blocks in the quilt on these pages are also made up of three fabrics: a blue print, a medium blue solid, and a dark blue solid.

One can only imagine the time and patience it took to piece the silk and velvet Stars and Hexagons on pages 58 to 59. For those whose aesthetic sensibilities are offended by the general lack of restraint in Victorian crazy quilts, this example will be refreshing: although the crazy appliquéd work is heavily embroidered, as was the custom, it is confined to the borders only. It could be that a crazy quilt top was cut up to make the borders; for one thing, something that looks like the front wheel of a bicycle can be seen at the bottom edge. The corner blocks appear to make use of a popular purchased needlecraft notion of the time, the pre-embroidered appliqué. Other smaller purchased appliqués are used in the border.

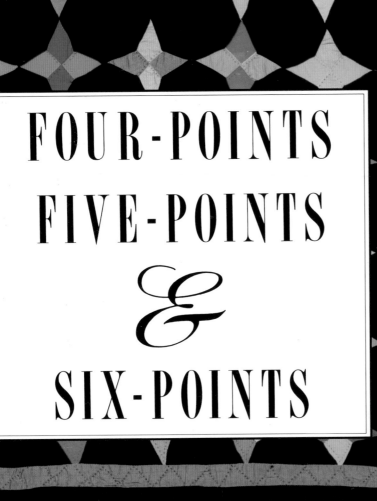

FOUR-POINTS
FIVE-POINTS
&
SIX-POINTS

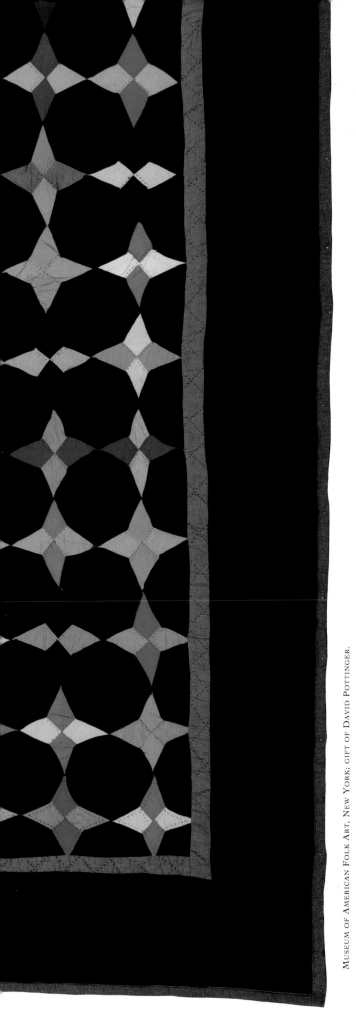

5

There exists a veritable gal-

axy of stars that have fewer than eight points. The chapter "Stars and Hexagons" introduced some of the six-points, but there is a wide variety of four-points and five-points as well. Interestingly, there are no seven-point star quilts that I have been able to find.

Six-point stars can be made using the pieced-diamond method described for Lone Stars. The star looks exactly like a Lone Star, except it has six points instead of eight. It is usually named Columbia Star, but sometimes it is called Star of the East. One variation of the plain six-point is Stars and Planets, which has quarter circles set between the star points. Barbara Brackman lists thirty-three different six-points in the section on six-point stars in her *Encyclopedia of Pieced Quilt Designs*, but there are additional ones elsewhere in the book, so the total is more than

PRECEDING PAGES — Simple four-point
stars glitter on a dark background.
*Amish, maker unknown; Shipshewana, Indiana;
c. 1925; 66 x 88 inches.* **A B O V E   A N D**
O P P O S I T E — It is difficult to believe that the
side and center panels of this quilt are
made from the same pattern. *Made by Lori Moore;
Pensacola, Florida; c. 1985; 69¹/₂ x 72¹/₂ inches.
Pattern on page 153.*

five-pointers is that the pattern is so difficult to draft from scratch.[8]) On those rare occasions when we find an appliquéd star, it is very often a five-point.

The four-point is as simple as a star can be, but the variations on it seem endless. The points can be placed on the horizontal and vertical axes of the block, or they can be placed on diagonal lines. The centers, where the four points meet, can have the bases fitted into one another, or the points can be arranged around a center square. That center square can be made of four triangles, or a square within a square, or a nine-patch. The star points themselves can be pieced of triangles or a combination of triangles and squares. Some of the wonderful names the four-points go by are World Without End, Crossed Canoes, and Rocky Road to Kansas.

The name of the quilt on the preceding page is fascinating: Black Hummingbird. The "humming-birds" are actually four-point stars, most of which have yellow "wings" or "bodies." There are some places where black fabric was used for two of the star points, and a different shape emerges, like two arrowheads placed with their bases touching. The 165 stars of the quilt have lots of twinkle power, due in large part to the dark background; interestingly, the border of the quilt is a dark navy, although the field of the quilt is black. Another name for this quilt is Snowball, although it hardly seems appropriate when the snow-balls are black.

If not for the center panel, it might take forever to figure out the basic building block of the quilt on these pages. It is nothing more complicated than a sim-ple four-point star, but it is done in three colors. In the center panel, the two strongest colors make the star points and a pale stripe is used for the background; sixteen small stars appear prominently. However, in the flanking panels a different color scheme places a dark blue in the background, so that a different star entirely emerges from the pattern. There appear to be four of these dark blue stars, surrounded by a circle of white, in each of the side panels. It takes real study to

that; a complete count is difficult.

Although everybody's favorite star to draw is a five-point, there are not all that many five-pointed stars on quilts. Most of them are found on quilts that have a patriotic theme, and nearly always the name applied to them is Texas Star. In the past, the five-point was also know as the Union Star. (The reason for the dearth of

ABOVE AND OPPOSITE — This quilt, so similar to the preceding one, is named Pine Burr. *Made by a member of the Baker family in Blount County, Alabama; c. 1875; 73 x 85 inches. Pattern on page 155.*

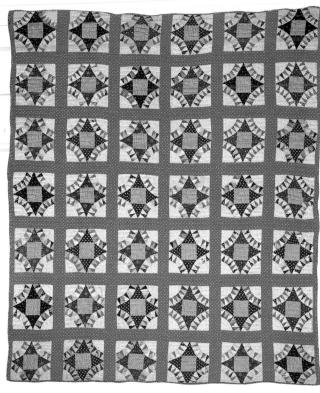

LEFT AND ABOVE — Feathered
edges on a four-point star create secondary designs
of circles. *Made by Rebecca Davis; Chambers County,
Alabama; c. 1870; 62¹/₂ x 72¹/₂ inches.*
OPPOSITE — A contemporary four-point star
quilt is named Midnight Stars.
*Made by Dixie Haywood;
Pensacola, Florida; 1980; 56 x 72 inches.*

element of the quilt top. This striking quilt is made
from myriad fabrics, although the quilter limited her
color scheme to blue and black for the stars, with the
same center in all.

Nine four-point stars "on point" make the center
field of the beautifully designed quilt at right. The center panel nestles into another large four-point, and the
top and bottom borders each contain seven more stars.
The border stars are the same as the ones in the central

panel, but they are not on point, and the fabric is
worked completely differently, so one gets the impression of a different star entirely. Midnight Stars is an
exercise in subtle blending of colors and prints.

Some of the most unique of all star quilts are
included in our collection of five-point stars. For example, the crazy quilt on page 74 is actually very well
ordered, not "crazy" at all. The black-and-white five-
point stars that swirl through each of the eight blocks

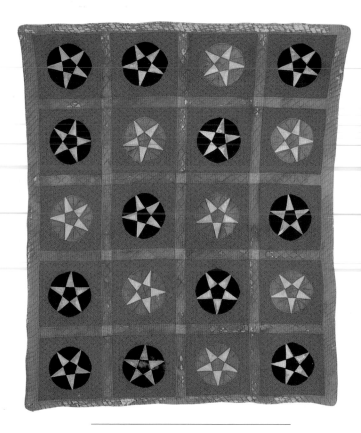

ABOVE — This five-point star is universally known as Texas Star. *Provenance unknown; c. 1875; 67 x 78 inches. Pattern on page 156.*

RIGHT — An organized crazy quilt features a number of five-point stars. *Artist unknown; found in New Hope, Pennsylvania; 1875-1900; pieced silk; 44½ x 80½ inches.*

OPPOSITE — A quilt block looks like a puzzle in which the game is to find as many stars as possible. *Provenance unknown; c. 1825.*

are in fact in orbit around a blue-and-red five-point that is placed in the exact center. Those seemingly amorphous shapes that fill in the block are identical in each block.

The center of the Texas Star is a pentagon, and slender points are arranged around its five sides. In this example, the pentagon is the same color as the background circle on which the star is placed, but often the center is the same color as the points.

Five-point stars and pentagons are a natural pairing in the quilt block at right. There are stars with red points and white centers on a white pentagon; there are those with white points and red centers on a red pentagon; and there is the big red star that is almost the same size as the block. The embroidered hearts are an odd decorative touch.

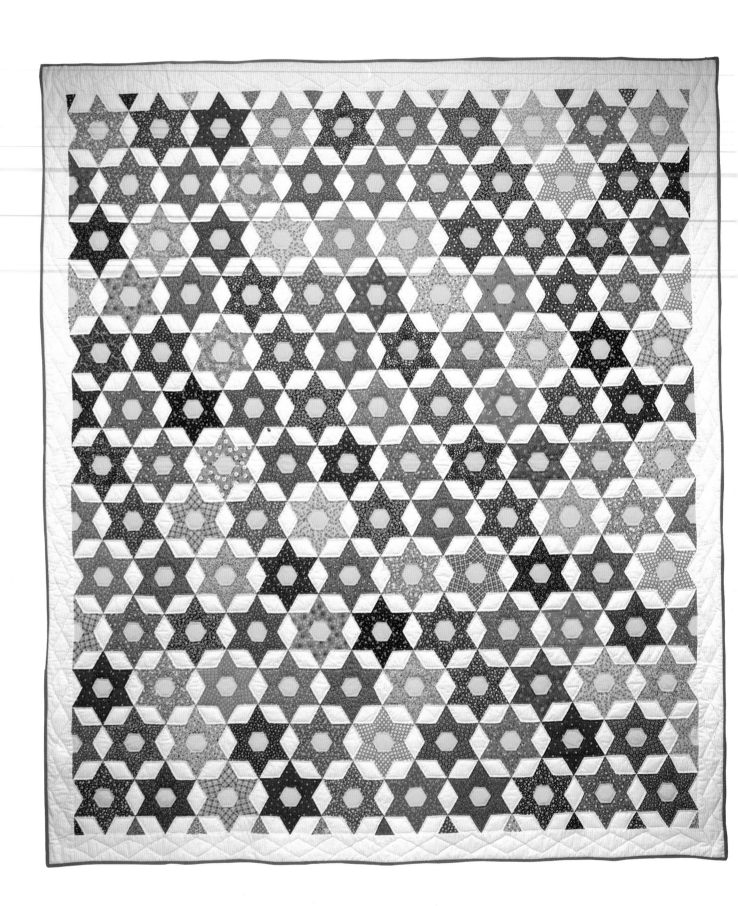

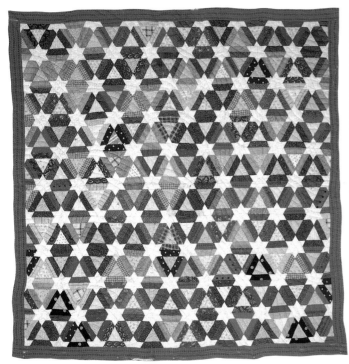 

OPPOSITE — This design was often chosen for
autograph quilts in the nineteenth century. *Made by Annie Lou Hanson;
Mobile, Alabama; 1984; 83½ x 95 inches. Pattern on page 177.*
ABOVE — Pairs of old quilts are rare; these are done in the
Smoothing Iron design. *Made by Belle Phillips Boyd; Upatoi, Georgia;
1890-1900; red-bordered quilt is 74 x 77 inches; blue-bordered one is
is 78½ inches square. Pattern on page 157.*

Although the six-point stars shown on these two pages are similar to those shown in Stars and Hexagons, pages 58 to 63, there are significant differences in the ways the stars are set together. In the quilt at left, the negative shapes between the stars appear as diamonds rather than hexagons, and in the pair at the top of this page, triangles are formed between the stars.

Six-point stars with yellow centers sprinkled gaily across the entire quilt surface inspired the name Star Flowers, at left. The petals are an assortment of bright calicoes, which will make a valuable resource for future generations who want to study late twentieth-century fabrics. This design was a popular choice for autograph quilts in the nineteenth century; a name

was written in the center hexagon. Each star was then placed in a block and the blocks were set together with sashing.

Pairs of old quilts are very rare; however, more pairs appeared after the advent and subsequent popularity of twin beds in the 1940s and 1950s. In this pair from the turn of the century, the same pattern and fabrics are used, but the quilts are of slightly different sizes; perhaps the beds for which they were made were not quite the same size either. The patterning is ingenious: triangles with white points are fitted together and six-pointed white stars are formed, more or less as lagniappe. The only name we have found for this quilt is Smoothing Iron, taken from an item all too familiar to the homemaker of the period.

6

Just as there are stars with

fewer than eight points, there are stars with more than eight points, and those are the ones I have classified as Blazing Stars. A quick glance might lead one to think that all the designs are those known as Mariner's Compass. Although Mariner's Compass quilts as a single type are probably more numerous than any other in this category, there are many stars with more than eight points that are not based on the compass rose. For example, thirty-two points can be counted in the Blazing Star on these pages; a layered sixteen-point star makes the Sun in the Adam and Eve quilt that follows. There are also twelve-point stars; many of them evolve from a six-point star and have a hexagon in the center.

Sun and sunflower names are often given to these many-pointed stars, with Sunburst being the

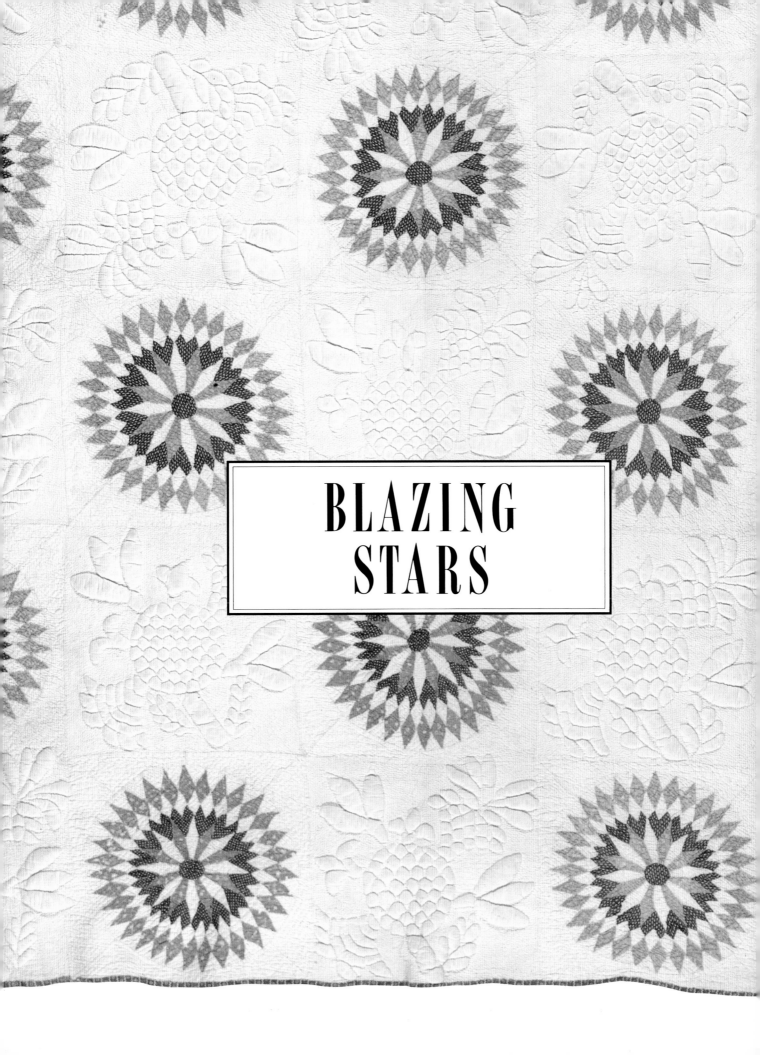

BLAZING
STARS

favorite for those with sixteen or more points. (The reader will recall another pattern named Sunburst from pages 38 to 39. There is no standardized nomenclature in quilts.) If the design has a large circle in the center, it has frequently been named Sunflower, and even more often Kansas Sunflower. Some other engaging names for Blazing Stars are Tropical Sun, Merry-Go-Round, Sunrise, and Noonday. Chips and Whetstones is another familiar name in this category; the quilts that most often bear this label begin from a basic star of six rather than eight points, but there are many secondary points in between the major ones. These variations will be viewed on the following pages, but first let us look at some true Blazing Star quilts, beginning with a close examination of the one at left.

Quilters have traditionally gone to the Bible for inspiration, but rarely is the result as urbane as this stitched story of the Garden of Eden. As in the well-known and more primitive Harriet Powers quilts, the purpose of this piece was to tell a story from the Bible. Whereas Mrs. Powers chose a single powerful image to represent the essence of the story, the maker of this quilt sequentially portrayed different scenes from the tale of Adam and Eve. The story begins at the left-hand side of the quilt. All is peace and tranquility in the garden—four birds are fluttering around the apple tree. The second frame of the story is at the bottom of the quilt, where Eve (fully dressed in nineteenth-century clothing) is taking an apple from the tree, while a serpent of monstrous size hovers menacingly near. Most of the birds and butterflies have gone. In the third scene, at the right-hand side of the quilt, Eve hands the apple to Adam, who appears as a black man who is not dressed at all; notice also that the tree has become diminished. In the fourth scene, Adam leads Eve out of the Garden of Eden. The double-trunked vine that begins at the bottom of the quilt was cleverly planned to be the fence—it provides the opening through which Adam and Eve are to be expelled.

The drama takes place around a central medallion that depicts the heavens. Included is a sun, made

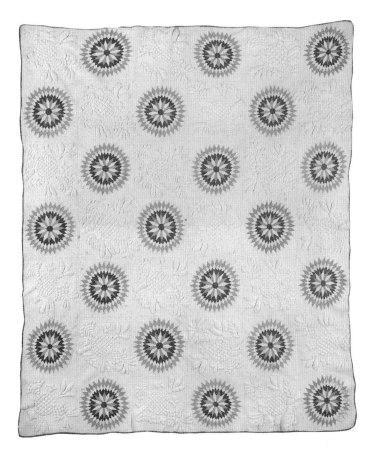

OPPOSITE — This incredible quilt, which depicts the story of the Garden of Eden, was bought at a church bazaar. *Maker unknown; found in Fort Smith, Arkansas, in 1900; c. 1850; cotton with some silk appliqué; 74³/4 x 85¹/2 inches.*
ABOVE AND PRECEDING PAGE — A Sunburst quilt is executed in the classic scheme of red, white, and blue. *Made by Elizabeth Taylor Brawner Perkins; Somerset, Kentucky; c. 1865; 74 x 86 inches.*

of a layered star of sixteen points; each layer is a different shape and a different color. Stars are pieced of eight diamonds and appliquéd in place. The four phases of the moon are rendered, with the new and the full moon identical. We do not often see in a quilt such a complete representation of the entire firmament.

The appearance is similar to the sun in the Garden of Eden quilt, but a different pattern is used for the Blazing Star above. Rounds of diamonds in increasing numbers make the pattern; it took thirty-two to make the outer round. The piecing is meticu-

ABOVE — This Chips and Whetstones quilt is often mistaken for a
Mariner's Compass. *Made by Olive Pool Reed; Boston or Easton,
Massachusetts; c. 1845; polychrome roller-printed cottons; 89½ x 95 inches.*
OPPOSITE ABOVE — One type of Mariner's Compass has a circle in the
center. *Made by Nancy Huibui; Mobile, Alabama; 1985; 36 inches square. Pattern on page 179.*
OPPOSITE BELOW — Another type of Mariner's Compass shows the
four-points fitted into one another at the center. *Made by Mary Chartier;
Gautier, Mississippi; 1981; 76½ x 98 inches. Pattern on pages 158 and 159.*

lous, even though diamonds of different sizes were used, and even though each motif forms a perfect circle. These circular motifs are but one indication that this was a best quilt, used only on special occasions, as when company came. When an elegant effect was desired, circular motifs were chosen, then widely spaced on a white background.[9] In this example, the quilting did not suffer a lack of attention; any open areas were stippled with stitches. The symbol of hospitality, a pineapple, was executed in stuffed work.

The primary difference between the perenially popular Mariner's Compass and the very old design at left, known as Chips and Whetstones, is that a Mariner's Compass is based on a four-point star, and Chips and Whetstones on a six-point star. The Mariner's Compass design was taken from the compass rose, a design perhaps as well known to the wives of seafaring men as to the sailors themselves. From the sound of the name, Chips and Whetstones had a different, more land-oriented beginning.

In looking at New England quilts that were inspired by the compass roses of old sea charts, Judy Mathieson discovered that "These quilt designs usually have sixteen to thirty-two points arranged in a circle with four of them more prominent than the others. They are also usually oriented in a square block with the prominent points in North, South, East, and West locations."[10] Further, she says, they have some kind of design in the center: circle, hexagon, etc. See above right for an example of this Mariner's Compass. The design is layered, with the top, light-colored, four-point star representing the cardinal compass points of north, south, east, and west. The second star in the layered design, the dark blue, points to the northeast, southeast, southwest, and northwest. The other layers indicate the remaining twenty-four directional points.

Although this particular block only uses four fabrics, the design can become very ornate when more points are added, a profusion of fabrics is used, and the center is embellished.

Judy Mathieson goes on to say, "There is anoth-

er design that is nearly always referred to as 'Mariner's Compass,' where the intersecting lines meet at the center. Usually this design has only sixteen points and the rays are split in half lengthwise with one side dark and the other side light."[11] An excellent example of the second type of Mariner's Compass is presented at lower right on page 83. This design is also a layered star, but because each round of points is done in the same fabric, there is no contrast.

A note on the construction of this second quilt: individual compass stars were machine pieced, then appliquéd onto the background square. The garden lattice sashing is an interesting setting for the quilt; the maker says her inspiration for it came from a quilt at the Shelburne Museum in Shelburne, Vermont. There are two blocks in which the star is tilted—surely a deliberate touch.

Other interesting interpretations of the Blazing Star defy classification. The design at right is known as Rising Sun, although this particular quilt has been called Bull's Eye. Very few of these quilts exist, as they are extraordinarily difficult to piece. It consists of concentric rows of diamonds and triangles that must be set together precisely, or the finished circle will not lie flat. The addition of pots of tulips at each corner is a captivating touch.

Sunflower is the name of the design at upper left. It has been embellished in the center with a dark brown square with elongated corners, known as a reel. This shape is found on big utility spools onto which rope or wire is wound; although the centers of the spools are round, the ends are shaped like this to keep the spools from rolling. Spools of rope were common

sights in early seaports, and although it cannot be proven that the quilt motif came from them, we do know that quilters were quick to adapt the shapes they saw around them to their fabric pieces. The reel is a motif that has found many applications in quilting; one often sees it coupled with oak leaves or tulips, placed at the tip of each corner.

The binding of the Sunflower quilt was applied by machine; this was often done, even when every other aspect of the quilt was hand-done. Not only did the machine eliminate the time it took to do an essentially boring job, it gave the quiltmaker the opportunity to display the fact that she owned one of these great labor-saving devices. Sewing machines were a status

symbol when they were first manufactured in the early 1850s; the cost was very high, as much as six hundred dollars or more.

Although the design at right on page 84 might at first look like a Mariner's Compass, closer examination reveals that the second round of points contains an extra piece at the base, in the shape of a wedge. This design has been variously called Setting Sun and Rolling Pin Wheel. It was used as the center block in an album quilt dated 1842, now in the textile collection of the Smithsonian. The sixteen patterned circles of this quilt have been inlaid, rather than appliquéd, into one continuous length of fabric—the block style was not used.

7

The quilts in this classifica-

tion are like Feathered Star quilts in that there do

not seem to be many of them, although they are

among the most beautiful of all star quilts. The most

popular of the grouped-star quilts is named after an

actual celestial phenomenon, the Pleiades, or Seven

Sisters, which is a cluster of seven stars near the con-

stellation of Taurus, the bull.

Although there are other grouped stars that are

not related to the Seven Sisters design, it is by far the

most numerous in this category. Most other grouped

stars look like a simple four-patch pattern with the

same little star repeated in each corner of the block.

Two exceptions appear on pages 92 and 93.

The stars of all the versions of the Seven Sisters

quilts are six-pointed and are set together either in a

circle or in a hexagon. Barbara Brackman records a

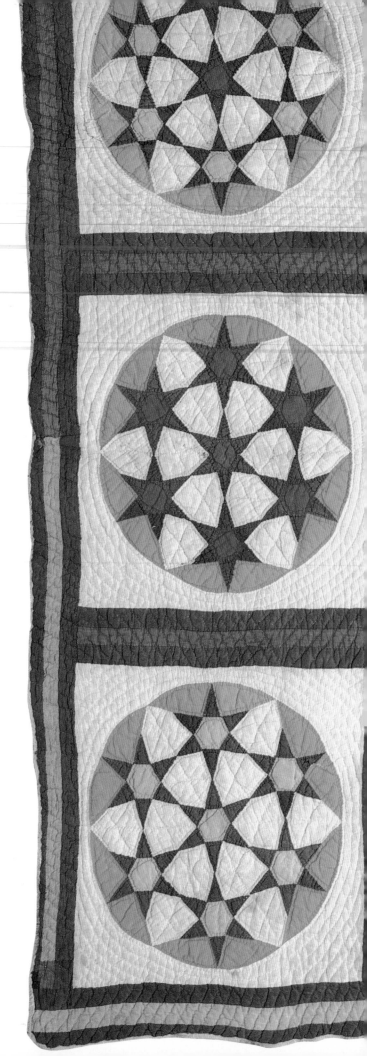

GROUPED STARS

dard references shows a Seven Sisters in a circular set, even though I found a number of actual quilts. Perhaps no pattern for Seven Sisters in a Circle was offered through the various magazines and newspapers consulted for those encyclopedic listings of quilt patterns and names.

Of all the Seven Sisters in a Circle that I found, the one on the preceding pages is unique. Bright little star shapes seem to be touching their points together to dance around a central star. The stars in this quilt have six points, and a hexagon appears in the center of each. The joining of the stars results in the formation of pentagons. The pentagons, in turn, form a six-petaled flower or star shape behind the seven dancing stars.

Country quilts are as indigenous to the southern rural landscape as the corn, sunflowers, and split-oak baskets that spring from this rich region. Quilts such as the one pictured here were often made from the flour and feed sacks that were part of country living. I can remember being allowed to choose, in the general store, the flour sacks from which my mother would make me a new playsuit, which she would eventually piece into a quilt. I have hesitated to share this memory because some readers might mistakenly think I had a deprived childhood; that is not the case at all. The flour sack fabrics were lagniappe to us; we were going to buy flour anyway, and we thought it was just terrific that the makers packaged it in wonderful cotton print bags!

The blocks in the Feed Sack Seven Sisters are set together with no sashing. An interesting secondary pattern is formed that resembles a six-pointed snow crystal. Each of the star clusters is finished so that it becomes a straight-sided hexagon; the hexagons are then sewed together to achieve the required length and width. Because everything is white but the stars and the binding, the stars appear to twinkle in circular clusters. An interesting secondary pattern resembling a six-pointed snow crystal is formed in the white areas.

The Seven Sisters in a Circle quilt done in a red, white, and green color scheme is substantially different

PRECEDING PAGES — An appropriate name for this quilt design might be Seven Dancing Sisters. *Maker unknown; Conecuh County, Alabama; c. 1875; 65 x 75 inches.*
ABOVE AND OPPOSITE — A Seven Sisters quilt of feed sacks is right at home with spilt-oak baskets and sunflowers. *Provenance unknown; thought to be from Lowndes County, Alabama; c. 1940. Pattern on page 164.*

Seven Stars set in a hexagonal shape from *Ladies Art Company*, published in 1898; the same pattern was called Seven Sisters when it was offered through the pattern service Mrs. Danner's Quilts sometime after 1934, and it was named Seven Stars in a Cluster in a 1928 edition of *Capper's Weekly*. The oldest recorded Seven Sisters quilt, again citing Brackman, is a quilt from about 1845 that appeared in *Quilt Engagement Calendar 1981*; that example also shows a hexagonal set.

It was surprising to find that none of the stan-

ABOVE — The Seven Sisters can be set into a hexagon.
Made by Ellen Mooty Enloe; Heard County, Georgia; 1883;
71 x 80 inches. Pattern on page 184.
OPPOSITE — These stars are made as though they were
cut with a cookie cutter–all from one piece. *Maker unknown;*
Madison County, Alabama; c. 1850.

from the Feed Sack Seven Sisters. One distinction between the two is that these stars are actually in a circle, rather than a hexagon. The Feed Sack Seven Sisters is put together very much like the quilt at left, although in appearance it has more in common with the quilt above. The use of sashing on the one above makes a little constellation of each little group, as opposed to the blending of all into a great Milky Way of the previous example.

Most remarkably, the stars are made from one piece of fabric and appliquéd in place. This is most unusual—six-point stars, indeed nearly all stars, are pieced, even in the rare instances when they are appliquéd onto a background fabric. This is a very rare variation of the design.

The quilt top at left is said to have been pieced by the maker when she was eight years old. It is an excep-

tional example, even for a more experienced needle-woman. It is a reflex response to doubt that someone so young could have completed something so complex; however, impressive accomplishments in many disciplines by children are reported and celebrated every day of our own lives.

Each hexagon is composed of seven two-color stars, some of which turn into "ghost" stars when they are too similar in color to the background. The dark green of the setting diamonds and borders contrasts sharply with other colors in the quilt. A whimsical note is the navy fabric printed with a pattern of white stars used for some of the pieces.

The innovative Double Star on page 92 breaks the rule that identical stars make a quilt design. A four-point is put next to a Star of Bethlehem in an unusual pairing that shows off each of the stars to fine advan-

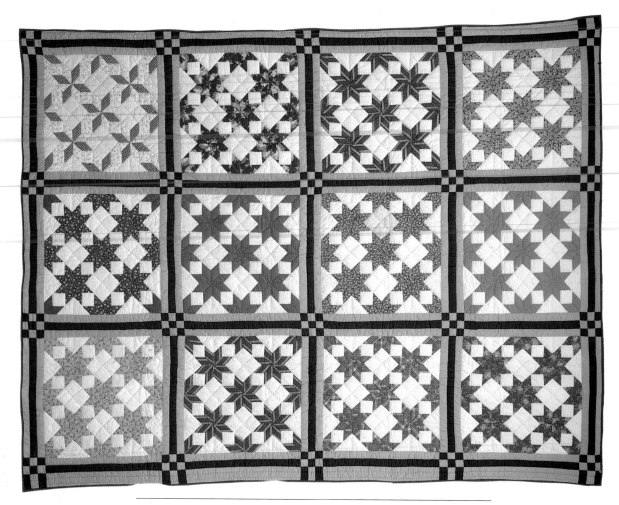

ABOVE — Numerous Stars of LeMoyne collected into a square
make a different type of grouped star. *Made by Emma Harmon and
Eugenia Lattner; Birmingham, Alabama; 1900; 65 x 86 inches. Pattern on page 170.*
OPPOSITE — An unusual combination of two patterns makes an original
quilt. *Maker unknown; thought to be from Autauga County, Alabama;
73½ x 77½ inches. Pattern on page 165.*

tage. The four-point functions as the setting block for the patterned Star of Bethlehem, or vice versa. The color scheme is mostly blue and yellow, although it contains scraps from just about every imaginable kind and color of cotton print—geometrics, florals, abstracts, paisleys. The maker skillfully placed the colors to create unity. She made the rows of four-point stars all blue on one row and all yellow on the next, both horizontally and vertically.

A final quilt leads us gracefully to the next chap-ter, presaging the versatility of the LeMoyne Star design. Five complete and several partial stars make up each of the blocks. The fabrics appear just as new and crisp as if the quilt were finished yesterday, although they all date from approximately the turn of the century. The sashing and nine-patch corner blocks add interesting finishing touches, as does the printed backing. There is a mysterious feature to the quilt: what could be the reason behind the wide stripe on one long border?

8

The Star of LeMoyne is one

of the oldest known quilt patterns, taking its name in America from Jean-Baptiste LeMoyne de Bienville and Pierre LeMoyne d'Iberville. The French Canadian brothers explored the coastline of the Gulf of Mexico from Pensacola to New Orleans, founding the cities of Mobile in 1711 and New Orleans in 1718; each went on to rule the giant territory of Louisiana, which would be purchased from France by the United States almost a hundred years later. The star named for them is thought to have first been used as a quilt motif in New Orleans, or possibly in one of the other successful French colonies that dotted the Mississippi River up to St. Louis. It is not surprising that the English chose to modify the name "LeMoyne" Star to "Lemon" Star: the LeMoynes were bitter enemies of the British for most of their lives.

STAR OF
LE MOYNE

PRECEDING PAGES — A large bicolored Star of LeMoyne is
enhanced by full and partial smaller stars in the same color scheme.
Provenance unknown; glazed cotton chintzes; 74¹/₂ x 76¹/₂ inches.
ABOVE — Stars of LeMoyne alternate with pink blocks for a
simple setting. *Provenance unknown; c. 1875; 67¹/₂ x 84 inches; 7-inch-square block.*
Pattern on page 141. *OPPOSITE* — Sashing and
corner blocks are another method for setting Stars of LeMoyne together.
Provenance unknown; c. 1920; 61¹/₂ x 80 inches; 8¹/₂-inch-square block.

The Star of LeMoyne is the simplest of star designs, consisting of eight diamonds fitted together. It is the basis for an extraordinary number of variations, and, in fact, a LeMoyne Star is formed at the center of all the stars in the Star of Bethlehem category. Of course, quilt terminology being what it is, this has meant that the Star of Bethlehem has been named LeMoyne Star and that the LeMoyne Star has been called Star of Bethlehem or Lone Star.

The examples presented on pages 94 to 107 are but a few of the many adaptations possible. All lily and peony and many of the tulip designs are based on the Star of LeMoyne. Carolina Lily, one of the oldest, and one of the few pieced flower designs, is based on half a Star of LeMoyne. Peony is similar to, and often confused with, Carolina Lily, but it contains six of the star points rather than four. Many basket patterns are also built on the Star of LeMoyne: Flower Basket, Basket of Scraps, and Cactus Basket are some of the familiar manifestations.

To duplicate any of the basic Star of LeMoyne designs, simply choose a 45-degree diamond in the size you desire from pages 140 to 141, cut eight of them, and sew them together. You must then finish the star into a block so that it can be set into a quilt; this is done by adding four squares for the corners and four triangles for the sides. The length of each side of the square is equal to the length of one side of the diamond. If you choose a diamond that has a 2-inch side, you will need 2-inch squares to finish out the design. The triangles are the same size as half the squares; however, the pattern piece is slightly larger than half the square because of the 1/4-inch seam allowance that must be included on the long diagonal side.

A pattern for a simple Star of LeMoyne is given on page 141; all Stars of LeMoyne are made the same way, with the same number of pattern pieces, no matter what their size. The diamond for the pattern on page 141 measures $1^3/4$ inches on one side; it yields a 7-inch square. Use this as a starting point to determine what size diamond you will need for your own star.

It is always a good idea to make a test block to check finished size.

Small stars of LeMoyne are prime candidates for hand piecing; see page 131 for specifics. See the instructions for "The Super Star—How to Make a Quilt Top in a Day" if you want to make a quilt with huge diamonds, like the one on the preceding pages.

The simplest treatment of the Star of LeMoyne occurs when all eight diamonds of the star are the same color and the star blocks are set alternately with unpatterned ones. The quilt at left contains sixty different blocks in which each star is made from one fabric. The backgrounds vary from star to star, but a peaceful, harmonious result is achieved through the use of the soft pink fabric as setting blocks. The pink becomes, in effect, the background for the field of stars. The simplicity of the quilt is further enhanced by the absence of any sort of border; even the binding is barely visible.

The powerful impression that a striped fabric can

ABOVE AND OPPOSITE — This Star of LeMoyne quilt is backed with feed sacks, with the original stenciling still visible. *Provenance unknown; c. 1910; 64 x 78 inches; 8-inch-square block.*

create can be observed in the four stars that were cut from a beige/brown stripe. The diamonds were placed randomly on the stripe; put together, they look skewed. It almost, but not quite, looks as though two fabrics were used.

The Star of LeMoyne can also be set with sashing and corner blocks. The gay combinations of fabric scraps make this a very cheerful piece. Another very effective way of putting the Star of LeMoyne quilt together is with the Streak o' Lightning set. See pages 36 to 37 for a quilt that utilizes this set, although with a different star.

An excellent example of a utility quilt is this scrap Star of LeMoyne sashed in red and backed with flour sacks. The term *utility* is applied to those quilts that were turned out for the practical reason that a warm cover was needed. They were made from scraps, as this one was. It is possible that the red fabric for the

OPPOSITE — A Touching Star of LeMoyne quilt incorporates an interesting quilting design in the pink blocks. *Provenance unknown; c. 1925; 65 x 85 inches. Pattern on pages 166 to 167.* *ABOVE* — Many types of stars surround the Star of LeMoyne center in this Victorian quilt. *Maker unknown; Kentucky; c. 1890; velvet with embroidery; 89 inches square.*

sashing was purchased specifically for this quilt, but certainly all the other material was recycled. The fabric for the backing must have been folded while the ink was still wet from the stenciling, since the stencil appears in reverse. One wonders what "F F" means — Fine Flour? Whatever it originally contained, the sack was intended specifically to be recycled as a sheet.

When Stars of LeMoyne are set together so that the points meet one another, they are called Touching Stars. In the example at left, the design has been manipulated to devise a sophisticated pattern that fools the eye. The stars are set on the diagonal, and the small blue squares that are placed where the tips meet are deliberately a different color from the print background, so that they act as a link between stars. In some colorations, Touching Stars look like twisted ribbon that is tacked on to the surface of the quilt.

A pieced Victorian quilt, above, provides the opportunity to compare several types of stars. The LeMoyne Star is repeated four times to make the central medallion. It also appears at the center of each side in the outermost border, flanked by Variable Stars that

have crosses worked in the center block. A border of Ohio Stars surrounds the central medallion, and each of their centers is a four-patch. The third border is made up of random patchwork squares, cornered with Ohio Stars. This quilt has the feeling of an elaborate tile floor—a design based, as these different stars are, on a square and its possible divisions. This quilt provides evidence that not all Victorian velvet and embroidery work was of the "crazy" style, although the vogue for that style did produce many more examples. This quilt is reminiscent of those made a century earlier that featured pieced borders surrounding a central medallion, in the English style.

Carpenter's Wheel is the name most often applied to the variation of Star of LeMoyne on these two pages. Its resemblance to two other quilt designs, the Broken Star (pages 28 to 31) and the Rolling Star (following pages), is immediately apparent. There is another design, not included in this book, that is often

confused with Carpenter's Wheel: it contains a pentagon between each diamond in the ring surrounding the LeMoyne Star and is more accurately named Star of the Magi.

It is not known where the name Carpenter's Wheel came from, although Ruth Finley uses that name for this design in *Old Patchwork Quilts and the Women Who Made Them*, published in 1929. Equally mystifying is another popular name, Dutch Rose. It is often called Octagonal Star, although that name better suits the quilt on page 106. It comes as no surprise that it has been named Star of Bethlehem, since that seems to be the label given every star design that wasn't called Variable Star! Perhaps the most romantic of the many different names it has had is Lone Star of Paradise, given to it in the *Kansas City Star* in 1933.[12]

The presentation at right, in which one motif is made large enough to fill the entire quilt, was named Black Diamond in a 1910 publication by Clara Stone called *Practical Needlework Quilt Patterns*.[13] The color scheme chosen by this quilter actually utilizes sixteen black diamonds, which raises the question as to whether or not the directions on the pattern included color suggestions. The illustration in Brackman's *Encyclopedia of Pieced Quilt Patterns* indicates that a two-color scheme was to be used.

An old, fragile Carpenter's Wheel on this page repeats the motif thirty-six times across the surface of the quilt. The shredded camel-colored fabric was most likely originally green; it is easy to imagine how spectacular the quilt was when new. The workmanship is of the finest quality, bespeaking the care that went into this piece.

Of all the quilts in this book, only one other has the "twinkle potential" of the Rolling Stars, two versions of which are seen on the following pages. That is the frontispiece quilt, and it should be examined in conjunction with the one on page 104. While the stars on page 104 seem to twirl, or roll, the frontispiece quilt, named Starry Paths, shoots out rays of color in all directions, making it one of the liveliest of all quilt

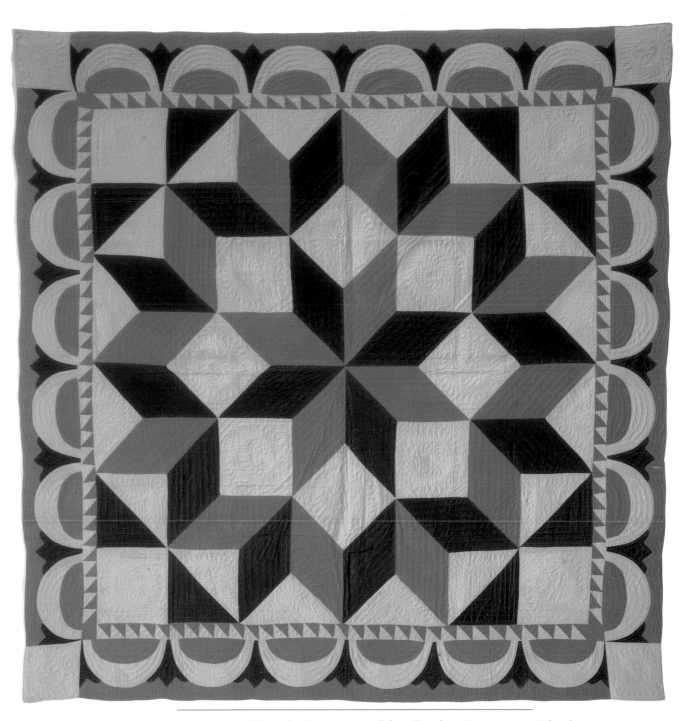

OPPOSITE — Although timeworn and fragile, this Carpenter's Wheel remains a telling example of fine needlework. *Maker unknown; southeastern United States; c. 1865; 75 1/4 x 82 inches. Pattern on pages 168 to 169.*

ABOVE — This quilt features one big Carpenter's Wheel as its central motif; interesting borders complete the design. *Maker unknown; Lebanon or Lancaster County, Pennsylvania; c. 1880–1890; 84 1/2 x 85 1/2 inches.*

ABOVE — Interesting adaptations such as the Octagon Star above demonstrate the range of the Star of LeMoyne. *Made by Isabella Fleming and Doris Boucher; Paducah, Kentucky; c. 1885; 81 inches square.*

35; although the design and the maker of the quilt are different from this one, the sashing is treated in the same way so this secondary design is formed.

The variations on Star of LeMoyne are practically endless. Not only is it one of the simplest of star designs, it is one of the oldest: the design has been in America for nearly two hundred years, and many quilters have set their hand to it over that time. Three unusual results of their efforts may be examined on these two pages.

It is easy to see what an appropriate name Octagon Star is for the design at left. A simple Star of LeMoyne is at the center of the quilt; the addition of a row of squares and a row of diamonds turns it into a Carpenter's Wheel. Multiple rows of squares and diamonds are finished off with half squares so that a smooth-side octagon is formed. What makes this design different from the Sunburst on pages 38 to 39 is that this quilt is made from two pattern pieces a square and a diamond—and the other quilt is made from just the diamond. The strawberry pink and green calicoes are two of the most popular fabrics in quilt history.

The LeMoyne Star takes on a floral feeling when it is surrounded by peony shapes (top right). Many names are associated with this pattern: Stars and Cubes, Yankee Pride, Maple Leaf, Cubes and Tiles, All Hands Around, Captive Beauty, Heavenly Stars, and Snow Crystals. The design is basically a Rolling Star with the addition of four diamonds at each corner. There are fifty-six pieces in this one block—not a good choice for the faint of heart!

Quilters are persistent in their quest for new designs, so it stands to reason that someone would embellish the eight integral diamonds of the Star of LeMoyne. The result is a design most often called Flying Swallows, although it has also been named Star Wreath when the internal circle of diamonds is made in green. In the Flying Swallows design, the cluster of three diamonds is always darker than the background into which they are set. It is best attempted when one has experience piecing.

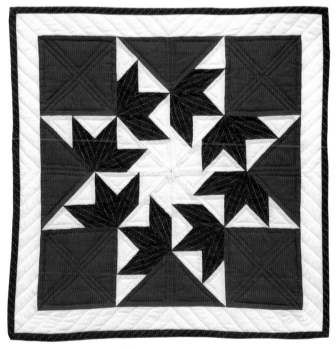

T O P — This design is very much like the Rolling Star, but there are extra diamonds at the corners. *Made by Margaret Livingstone; Mobile, Alabama; 1987; 14 inches square. Pattern on page 171.*
A B O V E — The diamonds themselves have been altered in the Flying Swallows version of Star of LeMoyne. *Made by Linda Dyken; Mobile, Alabama; 1987. 15 inches square. Pattern on page 186.*

9

Although all the quilts shown

thus far have featured stars as the main event, the "star of the show," as it were, stars are often supporting designs, accessories to the main theme. As we saw earlier, the first uses of the Ohio Star and the Variable Star were as border motifs on a medallion quilt (page 50). And, in addition to making exceptionally nice borders, stars are perfect design motifs for the corner blocks in sashing. They also fit nicely in the centers of Dresden Plate and Double Wedding Ring designs. In fact, stars pop up in a surprising number of unexpected places. The illustrations that follow are only the beginning.

For instance, almost every Princess Feather quilt contains a star. It is usually found at the center of the motif, where the plumes meet, but sometimes there are stars in other areas as well. The Princess

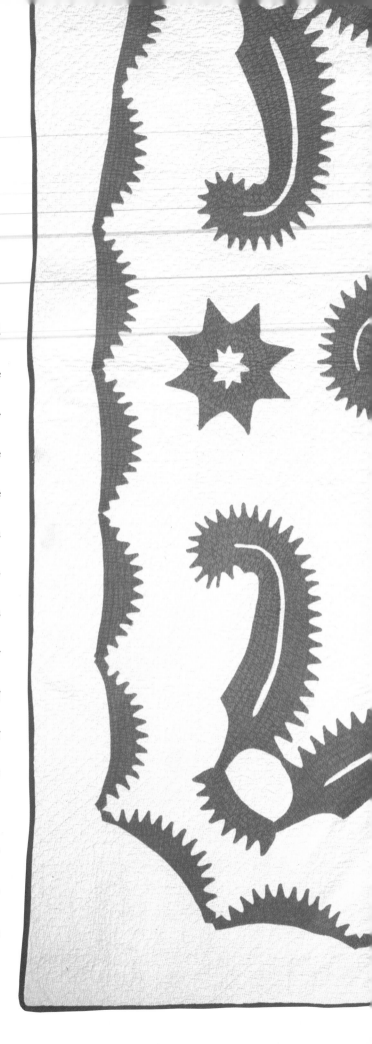

STARS
AS
ACCESSORIES

PRECEDING PAGES — A Princess Feather design has
rare appliquéd eight-point stars. *Provenance unknown;
c. 1840–1850; 81¹/₂ x 82¹/₂ inches.* *ABOVE* — In one of the most unusual
quilts ever, the star design is traced with bias tape. *Thought to have
been made by Louisa Hyatt Bynumm and/or her mother, Nancy Callaway Hyatt;
Blount County, Alabama; 72 x 96 inches.* *OPPOSITE* — The star
in the center of each block has worn away. *Provenance
unknown; c. 1840; 80¹/₂ x 75¹/₂ inches.*

Feather design was taken from the plumes on the Prince of Wales's ceremonial insignia, so the correct name actually is Prince's Feather. An interesting feature of the example on the preceding pages is the stylized crown at the base of the plumes in each corner; the person who made this quilt surely was aware of the royal connection. The stars themselves are interesting: although they contain eight points, they are not pieced. They are cut from one piece of fabric and appliquéd in place. A scalloped center has been cut from each.

The Prince's Feather and the Star of LeMoyne have always kept company. In a l941 article in *Woman's Day Magazine*, the author speculated that it was the attempt to duplicate a Prince's Feather by attaching

triangles to the edges of the Star of LeMoyne that produced the first Feathered Star.[14] The example above originally contained red plumes; those that now are white were originally colored; when the red fabric disintegrated, someone sought to extend the life of the quilt by simply removing the shredded fabric. The quilting is so well done that the quilt would be beautiful even if all the color provided by the appliquéd pattern were removed.

Stars are often found on quilts that have to do with plants and flowers, especially those that have a focus of growth and regeneration. On page 110, a Star and Tulip quilt explores the dual theme of planting and the heavens. Not only is the imagery compelling, the actual construction technique is fascinating. The star that forms the center of each motif was made by sewing bias tape in place as required to make the eight segments of the star and the stems of the tulip buds. The maker of the quilt cut yards and yards of bias tape and stitched as she went along, tucking and pleating the corners and points as needed.

The same idea of spring comes through in the quilt at right. The plant shapes appear to be sunflowers, and the red leaves look as though they are from the potato plant. The sun in the center reigns over all, and the border of redbirds and bluebirds adds to the sense of joy and contentment. The four groups of three stars each in the corners must have been put there to create the sensation of a sky. They are appliquéd five-points, with a hole cut out of the center.

The basis for the Reel and Tulip quilt below is an unusual striated chintz fabric. The background of the fabric is striped in dark and light values of the same color; this "rainbow" look was all the rage in fabric design during the first quarter of the nineteenth centu-

A B O V E — The blue print fabric used in this quilt was very popular in the early nineteenth century. Notice the Stars of LeMoyne in the sashing blocks. *Provenance unknown; c. 1830–1840; 86¹/₂ x 101 inches.*
O P P O S I T E — The owner of this quilt playfully christened it "A Twenty-one Bird Salute." *Maker unknown; found in Ohio; c. 1880-1900; 68¹/₂ x 87¹/₂ inches.*

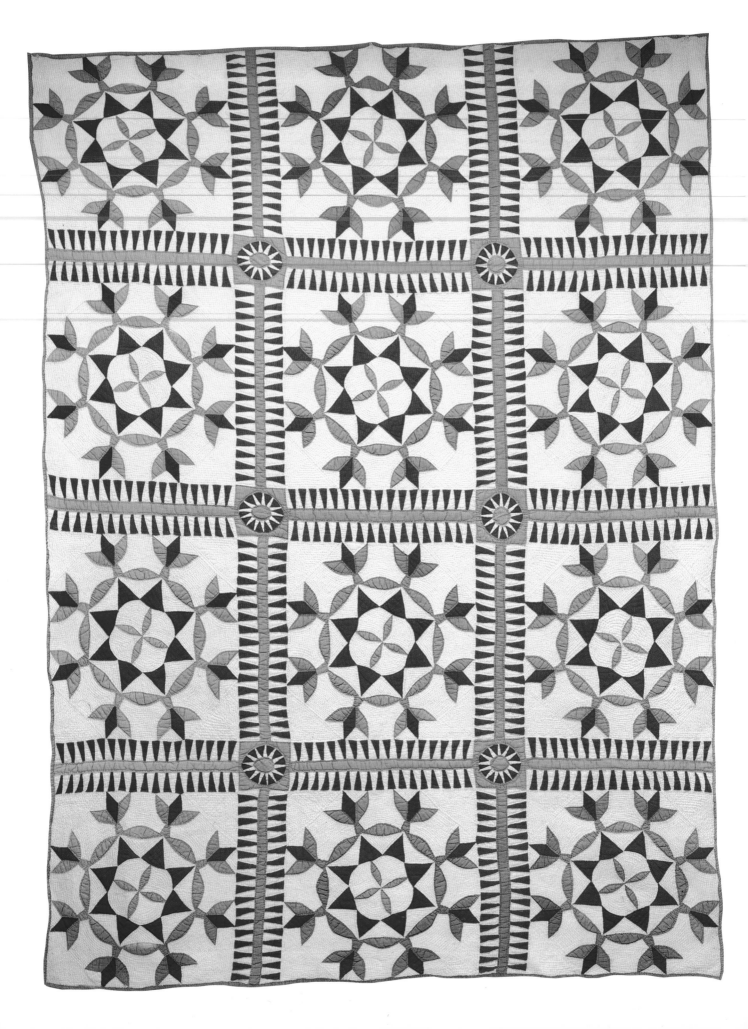

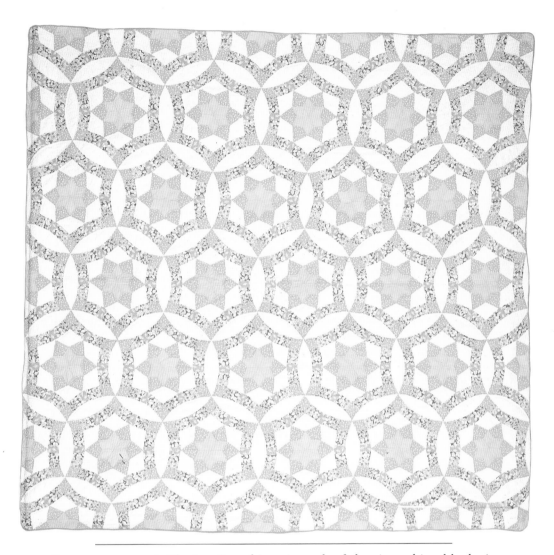

OPPOSITE — A Blazing Sun shines in each of the six sashing blocks in this original design. *Provenance unknown; c. 1840–1860; 69 x 93 inches.*
ABOVE — This Triple Wedding Ring is slightly different from its more familiar cousin. *Made by a Mrs. Sikes; Tuscaloosa County, Alabama; 1945–1950; 81 x 85 1/2 inches.*

ry. At least two and sometimes as many as three or four different colors could be used.[15] The extravagant use of the chintz, the choice of motifs with hard-to-make curves, and the sashing and star corner block suggest that this was a best quilt.

The quilt at left is the third in this chapter to celebrate springtime, growth, and regeneration. The four-branched leaf shape at the center of the block represents a seedling, and it is surrounded by an eight-point star or sun made from eight floating red triangles. A budding flower shape appears at the tip of each

of the red "sunbeams." The original green has faded to a camel color.

The Golden Wedding Ring above is a special quilt made in recognition of a couple's fiftieth wedding anniversary; a plain Triple Wedding Ring has no star in the center. The way to distinguish this pattern from the more familiar and the ever-popular Double Wedding Ring is to look at the shape that appears within the circles: if it has only four sides, it is a Double Wedding Ring; if it has six sides, the pattern is the rarer Triple Wedding Ring.

TECHNIQUES & PATTERNS FOR MAKING STARS

W hen you make a star quilt, you will use the technique of patchwork, rather than appliqué. It is much easier to sew diamonds together than to turn under seam allowances when the objective is sharp points and smooth inside corners. However, if appliqué happens to be your special love, take a cue from early quilters and lay on a motif from a chintz fabric at appropriate places, such as the inside corners of a big star, as in the example at right.

Hand or Machine Piecing?

Although machine speed piecing is the method of choice for many quiltmakers today, there are many people who enjoy hand-piecing, even though it's slower and to some minds, tedious. To those who love it, it is rhythmic and soothing. It is certainly more portable than machine piecing—you can cut all the pieces required for the entire quilt, separate them into individual blocks, and store each block in a self-closing plastic bag. If you make it a practice to take these bags with you, you can stitch over the course of a train ride, or a weekend, or a lunch hour, and you will have that quilt pieced before you know it!

Traditionalists who want their quilts to be like the earliest quilts will insist on hand stitching throughout. The sewing machine was not in general household use until the mid-nineteenth century, so all quilts before then were completely handmade.

The clever quilter will choose the technique according to the overall considerations of each quilt. If the purpose of the piece is to be a quick and colorful covering for a bed, for example, the logical choice will be machine piecing. If the quilt is a sentimental piece such as a marriage quilt, the maker might choose to do the entire work by hand.

Certain star patterns require familiarity with specialized techniques that go beyond the basics of hand or machine piecing, and these particular methods are explained on the following pages. First, though, let us set aside technique for a moment and think of procedure.

The Unit Method of Construction:

As anyone who's ever done any dressmaking knows, you work on one section of a garment at a time, finishing that section as nearly as possible before you attach it to another piece. Sleeve seams are sewn and the cuffs are attached before the sleeve is set into the arm-hole; collars are interfaced, faced, and pressed to perfection before they are attached to the neckline. This way of working is called the unit method of construction. There are many practical advantages to working this way: for one thing, all the pieces that belong to one section of the garment are kept together, lessening the chances for confusion; second, any problems with fabric, stitch length, or pressing can be solved on a small portion of the garment; third, it keeps bulky work at the sewing machine down to a minimum. These principles translate readily to the making of a quilt, most especially a patchwork quilt.

A quilt is made up of a number of units, called blocks, that are repeated over and over, with or without joining strips called sashing; borders may or may not be added, as desired. The blocks are sewed together sequentially, forming ever-larger sections of the quilt. The key to the entire quilt is the block that is used to make it. Become a quilt detective; examine quilts to see if you can pick out the blocks that were used to make them. Here are some clues:

★ There may be more than one block used to make the quilt. It is not unusual to find quilts that utilize two blocks, with two different patterns.

★ Sometimes the pattern is in the joining strips, or sashing. There are no rules about how wide the sashing may be, and sometimes the sashing is pieced and the blocks are plain. Storm at Sea, at right, carries the pattern in the sashing (the sailboats are the quilter's embellishment—they are not part of the original design).

★ Try to find the rows; watch for a diagonal set, which can be very confusing.

★ Look for the same shape repeated again and again.

★ The block may not always be a square. Rectangles are sometimes found; circular blocks are most often made into squares by the addition of borders.

★ Be aware that many times the quiltmaker was deliberately trying to camouflage or obscure the building block of the quilt by using color so that you see the overall effect instead.

Individual blocks also use the unit method of construction. Each block is broken down into a number of pieces that are regularly repeated. This is where the term patch comes in, as in a one-patch block, nine-patch, etc. The number of patches in a block is determined by the number of like, although not necessarily identical, units that are repeated to form the block. There are two-, three-, and four-patch blocks, as well as some with nine, sixteen, and twenty-five-patches. A nine-patch block, consisting of three rows of three identical units, was often a child's first piecing project. The plain nine-patch block is also frequently used at the intersection of sashing strips. A one-patch quilt is made up of one shape repeated again and again; the quilts in the chapter Stars and Hexagons are one-patch quilts.

The Unit Method Also Applies to Individual Blocks

Just as discovering the building block gives you the key to the quilt, the discovery of how the block itself is set together unlocks the secret of construction. Take, for example, the Ohio Star, which is a nine-patch block. It consists of three rows of three squares. There are, however, two different types of squares. One is unpieced and appears at the corners and the center of the block; the center square is a different color from the corner square. The other square is made of four triangles, two of which are the same color as the center of the block, and at least one of which is the color of the corner squares. Dissection of the block reveals that there are only two pattern pieces: a square and a triangle. The triangles make the star points in the design. This is the secret to the construction of every Ohio Star, no matter how small or large.

To apply the unit method of construction to the Ohio Star, you would proceed as follows:

1. Piece the units that make the star points: sew two triangles of different colors together, making eight pairs of triangles. Next, sew two pairs together to make one square. Repeat until four squares are made.

2. Study the star to determine how the squares must be set together into rows. The top and bottom rows are identical. Sew the blocks together to make those rows. Next, sew the remaining blocks together to make the middle row.

3. The final step is to sew the three rows together into your finished Ohio Star block.

OHIO STAR

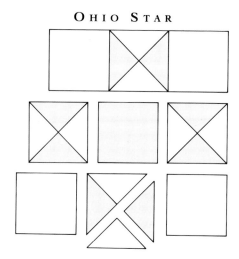

OHIO STAR
FINISHED BLOCK

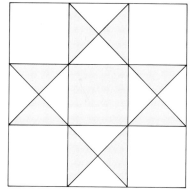

Let's do another, this time choosing a sixteen-patch star, the Variable Star. Two different kinds of squares make up this block, an unpieced one and a pieced one. Four unpieced squares are grouped to make the center of the star, and the pieced squares, made from two triangles, are arranged around the center to make the star points. The star requires eight unpieced squares and eight pieced squares. The steps, therefore, are:

1. Make the eight pieced squares by joining two different colored triangles.

2. Study the star to see how the squares are set together into rows: two different rows of four squares each are required for the block. The top and bottom rows are the same, and the two center rows are the same. Sew the squares together into the four rows.

3. Finally, sew the four rows together to make the block.

Sometimes the study of a block reveals shortcuts. For example, in the second example shown here, the units have been combined to save seaming. The corner squares are the same, but the four center squares have been cut as one piece. The points of the star are made by sewing two triangles onto one larger triangle; the seam that would have joined two squares has been eliminated. This technique of streamlining often works to improve the design; the central square in this star is much more attractive as a solid piece of fabric than it is with seams running through it.

VARIABLE STAR

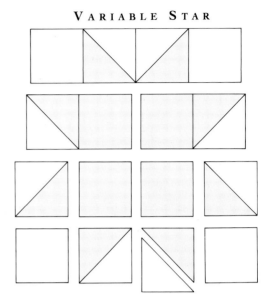

VARIABLE STAR
FINISHED BLOCK

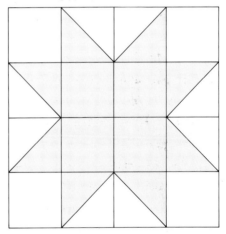

ALTERNATIVE VARIABLE STAR
FINISHED BLOCK

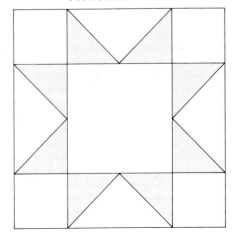

HAND-PIECING WITHOUT THE PAIN OF PUCKERS

O
ne enthusiast of hand piecing is Eunice Bush, who made the fabulous stained glass Broken Star on page 29.

At seventy plus, she's been piecing stars for more than sixty years, and here she generously shares her experience.

Planning the Colors

Eunice says this is the trickiest part of the entire project, but she believes "Either do not attempt it at all, or go through with it." In other words, "No intestinal fortitude, no glory." She always begins with a loose color plan, whether it be a soft pastel scheme, or one that uses only brights, or only primary colors, or tints and hues of one color. She chooses a selection of fabrics, and sits down at her worktable and "plays with them," placing one fabric against another until she gets a look she likes. She then cuts enough diamonds out to make one of the eight large pieced diamonds that comprise the large star and lays them all out and studies the effect. She substitutes fabrics until the colors and arrangement suit her eye, and makes a diagram of the large diamond, noting where each color goes. Finally, she counts the number of diamonds of each color so that she can go fabric shopping if necessary.

Cut the Pattern or Template, then the Fabric

Eunice stresses that your pattern must be completely accurate. She cuts several paper patterns at the same time, because the size can be diminished as she cuts close to the edge of the paper over and over. She checks her pattern for accuracy by aligning each of the four sides of the diamond with a straight edge. If one of the sides of the pattern is not perfectly straight, she discards the pattern, because lots of little tiny mistakes can add up to one big mess. Eunice most often works with a diamond that has 2" sides. If the quilt is to be very large, such as king size, she will move up to a 2 1/2" diamond, and/or she will make more rows in each of the eight large diamonds that make up the star. The diamond, no matter what size, always has l/4" seam allowances.

An alternative to a paper pattern is a plastic template. It is still a good idea to cut more than one template, because repeated use can alter the size and shape of even a plastic template. Cut it without seam allowances. Place the template on the wrong side of the fabric and trace around it with a permanent marking pen or pencil. This will be the stitching line of the diamond. Measure l/4" out on all edges of the diamond and draw a cutting line.

The point that Eunice believes in most fervently is positioning the pattern or the template on the grain of the fabric. She insists that the long direction of each diamond should be placed on the lengthwise grain of the fabric. This is a departure from conventional wisdom, which states that it is advantageous to place one edge of the diamond on the lengthwise grain, so that the cut diamond will have two parallel sides on the straight grain, which is the most stable direction of the fabric. The two other parallel sides are then on the true bias, the stretchiest direction of fabric. When the diamonds are joined, a bias edge will be sewn to a straight edge, and sometimes that just doesn't work well. You are, in effect, depending on the straight edge to stabilize the bias and prevent the stretching that would ruin the design. Eunice has found through trial and error that cutting the diamonds with the lengthwise grain results in less stretching, primarily because the edges are all the same; even though they are on the bias, it is not the true 45-degree bias.

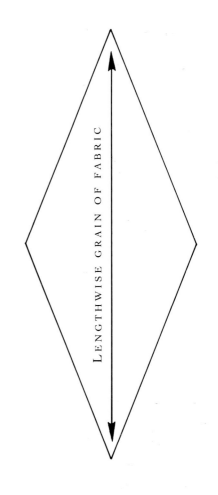

Stitching

The first step to accuracy is to mark the seam lines on each diamond exactly l/4" from the cut edge. If you use the template method described above, this will have been done. If you use paper patterns, you should mark with a straight edge and pencil or marking pen. The marked seam lines will intersect one another at the points of the diamond, and those intersections mark the exact end of the seam line. Without the marked intersection, it can be difficult to know where to start and stop sewing.

Eunice stitches the diamonds together into rows, placing the colors together according to her color placement diagram. She works on one-eighth of the big star at a time, putting the pieces for each of the eight big diamonds into separate plastic bags, and withdrawing

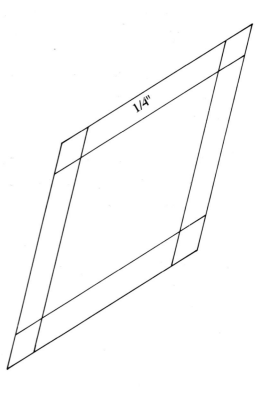

enough diamonds for one row at a time. The rows will have the same *number* of diamonds, but they do not have the same *colors* of diamonds. Use a small running stitch of at least 10 stitches per inch. Fewer stitches per inch will not provide a durable joining. Secure the beginning and end of each seam with a backstitch in the same place as your first stitch. Press all the seam allowances in one direction, toward what will be the center of the star, so they lie flat.

Pin the rows together, taking care to match the seam lines of the diamonds exactly from one row to the next. Once the rows are stitched together, you will have completed one-eighth of the star. Press the seam allowances of the rows all in one direction.

Sew the eighths together, two at a time, carefully matching the seamlines of the diamonds from one row to the next. *Always stitch from the center of the star out.* Once the eighths are joined to make quarters, you will join the quarters to make halves, and the halves to make a whole. Press the seam allowances all in the same direction. They will look like a little pinwheel at the very center of the star when they are pressed correctly.

Once the star is constructed, it is time to set the side triangles and corner squares in. Although all the points of the star are supposed to be the same length, they may not be exact, so you should measure and cut each triangle and corner square individually. Stitch the triangles and the squares into the inside corners by beginning at the inside corner and stitching to the tip. Do this in two steps, one for each side of the triangle or square.

Now your star quilt top is finished! But if it doesn't lie completely flat, Eunice says not to worry, it will flatten out when you quilt it. (Again, this is counter to conventional wisdom that says if the star is not flat when you finish piecing it, you might as well throw the quilt top away.) However, she does have one little trick to help flatten the star; she goes back to the seam in the area where the star is puckering and takes in just a needle's width wider seam, which tightens up the diamonds in that area ever so slightly without distorting them.

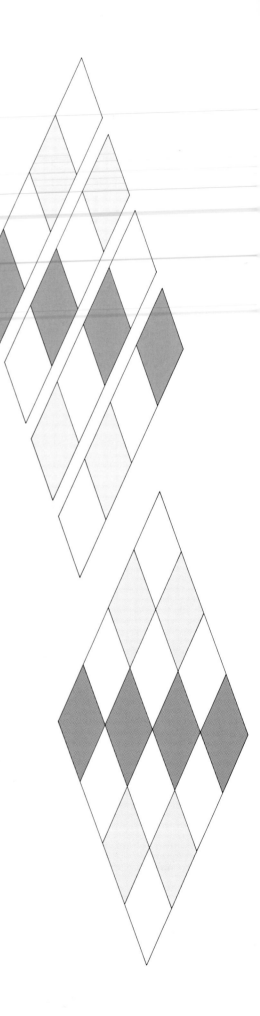

MACHINE-PIECED LONE STAR, BROKEN STAR, AND STAR OF BETHLEHEM

First and foremost, understand that you do not cut out one single diamond in this method! You do not need a diamond pattern or template. It's all done with strips of fabric sewn together in the width you want your finished diamonds to be.

You will need a rotary cutter and mat, and a no-slip ruler that has a least one diagonal line marked on it at a 45-degree angle (a 45-degree diagonal runs from corner to corner through the center of a square). Quilter's Rule is one of the many brand names for this type of ruler.

(*NOTE*: Scissors can, of course, be used to cut bias strips. Mark strips with a ruler and marking pen in the required width on wrong side of fabric, making parallel lines on the true bias. True bias is 45 degrees to the lengthwise and crosswise grain of the fabric.)

Planning Colors

The best way to decide on your colors is to have a general idea in mind and experiment on one segment, that is, one-eighth, of the star. Buy half yards of several fabric colors, and arrange them until you have the placement of color and pattern that suits you. Examine the color photographs to see how the final appearance of the star will be affected by the color arrangement within the individual segments— do you want your colors to repeat from the center in concentric circles, or do you want the center of the star to be different from the tips? You might even want to cut some strips out of the different fabrics and lay out one quarter of the star to check the repeats and overall pattern. Sometimes you come up with an entirely different color plan from what you thought.

When you have made a decision, draw up a diagram of one-eighth of the star and label your colors on the diagram. It is helpful to trace the diamond on page 138, adding or taking away rows to suit your design, and labeling it with your colors. Each of the rows that make up the one-eighth star must have as many diamonds as there are rows. If there are six rows, there must be six diamonds in each row; the rows are all the same length. The rows can contain even or odd numbers of diamonds; as few as three rows of three diamonds will produce a perfectly beautiful star, if fabrics are carefully chosen and coordinated. You may decide that the individual diamonds will need to be larger, say 3" instead of 2", if you want to use three rows of three colors. The larger unit diamond will, of course, result in a larger star.

Cutting the Pieces

Study your diagram to determine the color sequence of each row in the big diamond. Also count how many times the same row appears in the diamond. If you are working with four or six colors, you will see that two of the rows have the same colors in the same order, only reversed. So you can sew the strips for those rows and reverse the rows of diamonds after you cut them out.

Cut strips of fabric to the width that you want the diamond to be, plus 1/4" seam allowances. For example, if you want a finished diamond that has 2" sides, you must cut the strips 2 1/2" wide. Sew the strips together into rows, placing the colors next to one another as indicated by the diagram. You will have several different units of fabric, each containing different configurations of color, one for each row in the diamond.

1

1. Using the rotary cutter and mat, place the ruler across one end of one of the strip units, and make your first bias cut. Align the 45-degree mark on the ruler with the straight edge of the strips to get the true bias. Always hold the rotary cutter so that the screw that holds the blade in place is away from the ruler. After cutting off the end of the unit, continue cutting your strips of diamonds, making them the width of the finished diamond plus 1/4" seam allowances.
Cut all the color units into strips of diamonds, and refer to your diagram to see how many strips you need for each big diamond. Separate the diamond strips into those required for each big diamond, and store them together.

2. Lay the big diamond out, placing the rows next to one another in the order they should go. Pin the first row to the second row, right sides together, matching seam lines.

3. Take the pinned rows to the sewing machine, and lay the subsequent rows out in the order they should be added.

2

Sew the pinned rows together, then sew each subsequent row on, making certain that seam lines match and checking to make sure that the correct color sequence is maintained.

4. When the eight big diamonds are constructed, sew them together into twos, then fours, then sew the two halves of the star together to finish it.

The side triangles and squares are inserted after the star is finished. The length of the star point is the same as one side of the square or one side of the triangle. Measure the star point and cut the squares and fill-in triangles to fit. Do not forget the seam allowances. Sew the squares and triangles into the star by stitching from the inside, or the joining of the star points, to the tip of the point.

3

4

MAKING A BORDER OF DIAMONDS

A border of diamonds is very easy to make; you simply repeat selected rows from your big star, and they can be made by hand or machine. In Photo 4 above, the beginnings of a diamond border are lying end to end near the pincushion. The diamonds can follow one another all in the same direction, or you can plan to have the diamonds coming in from opposite directions to meet in the center, as in the example at right on one of Eunice Bush's quilts. She places two additional diamonds at the joining of the rows to make a graceful connection. A triangle can also be used at the joining.

FEATHERED STARS:
SIMPLIFYING THE "FEATHERS"

The most outstanding feature of feathered stars, and indeed, the characteristic that gives them their name, is that wonderful edging made up of tiny triangles. Each point of the star is outlined with these extravagantly pieced strips. It is the making and integrating of these strips into the design that requires thought and time, although the process is simpler than it used to be.

The first question you must ask yourself is: Are the legs on my star points the same length? If they are of different lengths, they may require two different size triangles to make the feathered strips fit the point exactly. Once you know what to expect, you will recognize why a pattern may have two triangles that come within 1/16" of an inch of being the same size. Not enough difference to worry with, you might be tempted to say. But stop and think: four of those triangles would make 1/4" difference in overall length when seamed together, enough to make or break a perfect fit.

Traditional hand piecing methods require a template for each pattern piece, and the required number of pieces had to be cut for each feathered star. Today's speed piecing techniques not only cut down on sewing time, they cut down on the number of pattern pieces. And that's wonderful news—even the simplest of the feathered stars, like the one on pages 42 and 43, requires 114 pieces for one block!

Speed piecing the feathers refers to the sewing together of the two different colored triangles that make the tiny squares which form the borders of each star point. Traditional hand methods involve cutting each triangle separately, then sewing them together to form a square. Even if the triangles are sewed together on the sewing machine, the cutting and matching up that must precede the sewing makes for very tedious work. The theory of speed piecing is based on sewing the seam first, then cutting the square. There are two methods; the results are the same in each. One method involves bias strips and is particularly suited to small pieces; the second method utilizes rectangles of fabric on which squares are drawn, and is a better method for larger sized pieces. These methods are for right angle triangles only.

Bias Strip Piecing

The first step is to determine what size square you will have after you sew together the two different colored triangles of your feathers, so that you can make your template. Measure one of the short sides of the triangle. That measurement is the same as the sides of the square. Make a template that is the same size as the finished square plus 1/4" seam allowances. For example, if your square will be 1" finished, your template should be 1 1/2" square.

The second step is cutting the bias strips of fabric. Place the two colors of fabrics right sides together, preferably on a cutting mat. Using the Quilter's Rule and a rotary cutter, cut bias strips in the quantity needed for your project. The width of the strips are determined by the size of the square: 2"-wide strips will be adequate for any of the feathered stars in this book. The length of the strips is determined by the individual star: two yards will be adequate for most feathered stars, but if the star is large, you might want to make three yards. This amount is a per star count; multiply by the number of stars to be made.

Sew the bias strips together by placing right sides of the fabrics together and machine stitching along one long edge. Do not stretch the bias as you stitch, and keep to an accurate 1/4" seam. Press the strips and the seam open and flat.

Working on the right side of the sewn strip, place the template for the square on the seam so that diagonally opposite corners are lined up exactly on the seamline. Trace around the template, then move it and trace another square directly next to the first, continuing the length of the strip. Several strips may be needed to obtain enough triangles for your project.

Cut the squares out, carefully following the marked lines. These squares will be sewn to one another as needed for the feathers. If you find that your pattern requires two different size feathers, keep them separated and identified in self-closing plastic bags.

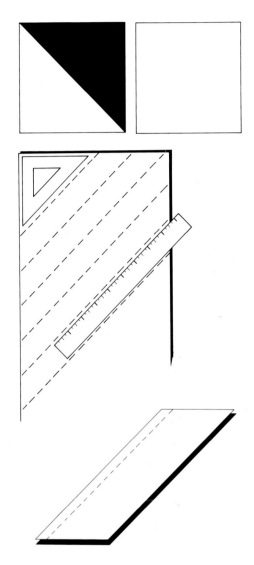

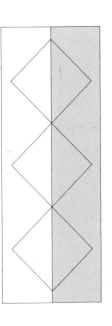

Drawn Squares on a Rectangle of Fabric

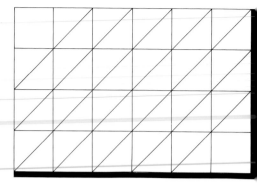

The first step in this method is to determine the size of the finished square: it will be the same as one of the short sides of the feather triangles. To the finished size of the square, add one inch. For example, if your finished squares are to be 1", you will need to draw 2" squares. Count the number of squares you will need. Keep any different sized squares separated from one another.

Work with rectangles of fabric that are about a half yard long and a half width wide (approximately 18" by 22"). Anything larger gets too big to handle easily. Use a fine-lined ballpoint pen or marker and a ruler that grips the fabric, such as the Quilter's Rule.

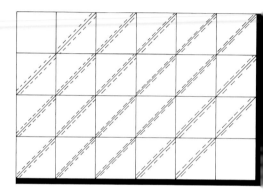

On the wrong side of the lighter colored of the two fabrics, mark a grid of squares in the size figured above; our example calls for 2" squares, so you would draw the horizontal lines 2" apart, then the vertical lines 2" apart. Next, draw one set of diagonal lines across the fabric that go precisely through each intersection of horizontal and vertical lines.

Place the right side of the marked rectangle of fabric to the right side of the unmarked rectangle of fabric. Pin the two together, keeping the pins away from the diagonal lines. On the sewing machine, stitch exactly 1/4" on both sides of the diagonal lines, using a 12 to 15 stitch length. It is easiest to stitch all the lines on one side of the diagonals first, then go back and stitch all the lines on the remaining side. If your presser foot cannot be used to accurately gauge a 1/4" stitching line, mark the stitching lines with a non-permanent marker or with stitching tape.

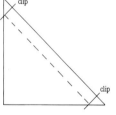

Cut through both layers of fabric on every one of the lines that you drew. You will have a number of squares, each made of two triangles, all exactly alike.

Before you press all your little squares, clip off the corners at the end of each seam. Open the square and press it flat, pressing the seam allowances open.

HAND-PIECING THE EIGHT-POINT STAR OF LEMOYNE

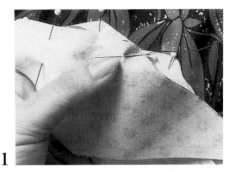

There are times when it is actually faster to just stitch your star up by hand than to use the sewing machine. This is especially true of very small stars that would be tedious to pin, then fit under the presser foot, and also when you are working with a fabric such as a stripe that could slip off match as it was machine stitched.

There are two ways to go about putting an eight-point star together by hand. You can sew two diamonds together to make a pair, sew two pairs together to make half a star, then sew two halves together to make a whole star. Or, you can pin all eight diamonds to one another, side by side, and sew them together, then sew the last two edges together to complete the circle of diamonds. Some people prefer to do all the pinning at once, and so prefer the second approach. The method of stitching is the same in both cases.

1. Start at the outer corner, or widest part of the diamond. Take your first stitch exactly on the seam line and secure it with a backstitch.
2. Stitch toward the tip of the diamond. About halfway down the side, take a backstitch, just to make the seam more secure.
3. Take several stitches on the needle at once. It speeds up your handstitching, and also makes the stitches more uniform.
4. Stitch to the tip of the diamond and secure with a couple of backstitches.
   Sew each of the eight seams of the star in this manner.

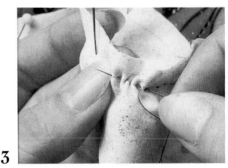

5. Take the following steps to ensure that you won't have a little hole at the center of your star: after matching all the seams to one another exactly and pinning, take a stitch through all layers of the star at the exact tip of the diamonds—go back and forth through the center several times. Next, without cutting the thread from the previous stitches, take a backstitch at the tip of each diamond. Continue around the star, taking a stitch between each point. Take two or three backstitches to end the stitching.

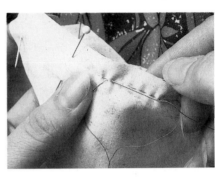

THE SUPER STAR:
QUILT TOP IN A DAY

The Super Star is a Star of LeMoyne made large enough to cover an entire quilt top. It is the star used to make the lovely Striped Star quilts, although its use is by no means limited to one style of quilt. The Super Star is the method by which you can duplicate a quilt like the big Star of LeMoyne (page 95), or any quilt made of diamonds too large to be printed in a book this size. It is entirely possible to draw the pattern, cut the pieces, and sew the star, complete with borders, all in less than a day.

Making the Pattern

The first thing is to make the paper pattern. Choose a stiff tissue paper that comes on a roll, in order to have the size you need. Use a permanent marking pen. A large-size cutting mat, while not absolutely necessary, is a wonderful help. You must have a heavy transparent rule, at least 24" in length, with the exact 45-degree diagonal marked on it.

1. Decide on the length you want each side of your diamond to be. Be sure to include 1/4" seam allowances. Draw a straight line to equal that length at one end of the tissue. With your ruler, draw the second side of the diamond: align the diagonal marking on the ruler with the first line you drew. That will put the long edge of the ruler at the 45-degree angle. Draw the second side of the diamond the same length as the first (Photo 1).

2. Draw the third side of the diamond the same way as the second side; finish the diamond by drawing the fourth side (Photo 2).

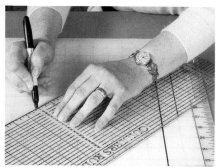

1

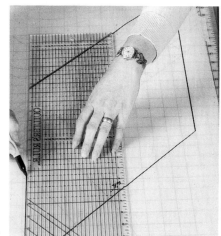

2

3. Mark the exact center of the diamond by drawing a line across it at the widest part. Label the diamond with all the information at hand. You will not remember details later. It is helpful to add a note later about the quilt you made from the pattern, whether it was the brown striped star, or the red and gold Star of LeMoyne, etc.

4. Now draw the fill-in half squares and squares that will finish off the Super Star. Work off the original diamond, using two different sides of the diamond as sides of the half square and the square. This ensures that the fill-in pieces will fit exactly. Begin with the half square. Place the ruler at the center mark of the diamond so that the diagonal marking aligns with one side of the diamond. Draw a line the same length as the side of the diamond (Photo 3). (NOTE: The label on the large diamond says: "16 1/2" diamond. Cut 8. Seam allowances included. Do not add.")

3

5. Connect the tip of the diamond to the end of the side of the half square. Draw a line with arrows to indicate the preferred grain line of fabric, and label the half square.

6. Draw the square by measuring straight out from another side of the diamond for two sides, making them the same length as the side of the diamond. Complete the square by drawing the fourth side and labeling (Photo 4).

4

The pattern is complete. Cut the tissue pattern pieces apart.

Cutting and Sewing the Star

Work with the fabric unfolded to a single thickness.

1. Begin by cutting away a length of fabric to be used for the border on the completed quilt (Photo 5). Put the border fabric safely away so that you don't mistakenly use it for another purpose. We used a rotary cutter on a cutting mat; you may, of course, use conventional scissors.

2. Place the diamond pattern on the striped fabric with the widest part of the diamond on the stripe you want to emphasize most. Cut eight diamonds, placing the pattern on the fabric in exactly the same manner each time (Photo 6). It is not necessary to pin the pattern on the fabric. Simply place your heavy ruler on the edge of the pattern, and hold it firmly in place while running the rotary cutter along the edge of the ruler (Photo 7).

The tip of the diamond may go into the selvage if necessary (Photo 8), because it will not show when the star is stitched.

3. After all the diamonds are cut, check to make sure that the stripes match exactly from one diamond to the next (Photo 9). Check all the diamonds, working in pairs.

4. Pin two diamonds to one another, matching the stripes exactly (Photo 10).

5. Starting at the outside corner of the pair of diamonds, lower the needle at the exact spot where the seam lines intersect (Photo 11). Always sew from the outer corner at the widest part of the diamond to the tip.

6. Stitch to the tip of the diamond, and secure the seam by backstitching two stitches (Photo 12).

7. Sew the diamonds into pairs, then sew two pairs together to make fours. Press all seam allowances to one side, in the same direction around the star (Photo 13).

8. Sew the two halves of the star together, sewing from one outside corner through the center to the other outside corner (Photo 14).

9. Press all the seam allowances in the same direction. Those at the center of the star will form a little pinwheel shape (Photo 15).

The star itself is now complete and ready for the addition of the half squares and corner squares. Pin each in place, one at a time, and always stitch from the widest part of the star toward the tip.

Small Striped Stars

If you want to make the smaller striped stars shown on this quilt, you can do so from the scraps. First, pick a diamond in the size you want from the selection on page 140. Make a template out of a material that you can see through, such as clear plastic. Take your template and place it on the stripes so that you make as many different stars as the fabric will allow. Always make sure you get eight identical diamonds so that your little star will be perfect, but don't worry about grain line of fabric. Place your diamonds lengthwise, crosswise, or diagonally as needed to get new stars. See if you can get the number of stars that you want without repeating the same design (Photo 16). It's a good idea to trace around eight like diamonds, so that you have a complete star, before you move on to the next star. Although the smaller stars can be stitched by machine, they are very easy, and probably quicker, to sew by hand.

5

6

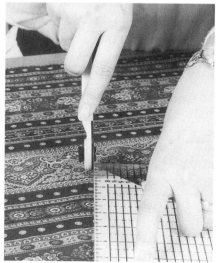

7

THE PATTERNS

There is an old Japanese proverb to the effect that if you give a man a fish, he eats for one day, but that if you teach him to fish, he eats for a lifetime. There is a similarity between that thinking and the idea that if you understand how quilts are put together, you have the knowledge to duplicate any quilt you see. Quilts are made up of units, called blocks, that are repeated a specified number of times (see The Unit Method of Construction, pages 119 to 121). On the pages that follow, you will find the pattern pieces needed to make one block of certain quilts that appeared earlier. The number of times that you make the block will be determined by the size of the quilt you are making and how you plan to set the blocks together.

The selection of patterns is representative of the wide range of stars, so that even if the pattern is not given for a specific quilt that you admire, you can use a similar pattern as a departure point to make the exact quilt that you want. Study the one in the book and see how it needs to be modified to give you what you want.

Don't hesitate to take what you need from different patterns to get the result you want. Also, you might want to try combining blocks in new ways to make a special quilt; an excellent example of the way this works is the "Double Star" at right (shown in color on page 93).

Please, please, note this word of caution: *make a test block of any pattern you choose.* The patterns are accurate when we draw them, but the mechanical processes that a piece of art must go through before it appears in this book may cause some distortion. Although it may be only minor, it can be enough to keep pieces from fitting together exactly. A test block will tell you what the demands will be on your technical skills to produce the particular design. You may find that the design is too easy, or that it takes more time than you want it to, or that you want to make it in a different size than you originally planned. It is also a good idea to try out the fabric and the colors you have chosen to see if you like them. There are innumerable reasons to make a test block; the lagniappe is that your test blocks can go into a fine sampler quilt.

Once you are satisfied with the block you have chosen, you can make the specific decisions that pertain to material requirements for the item you want to make. Your test block serves as a gauge for figuring fabric yardage in that it tells you how many pieces of each of the different fabrics is required.

The best way to accurately figure fabric yardage is to draw a cutting diagram for your project; it will be very similar to the cutting diagrams included in dress patterns. One good way to begin a cutting diagram is to figure out what the longest piece in each fabric will be, and use that as the length measurement of your fabric (this will be the number of yards to buy). For example, the longest pieces in all full quilts are the side borders. Working with a piece of graph paper in a scale that accomodates your project, mark off the length of the side border in one direction to make one side of a long rectangle. Use a width measurement of 45", as that is the standard width of most fabrics. Be sure to allow a 1/4" seam allowance on all edges of the border strips, and on any other pattern pieces that do not have seam allowances included. If your borders are to be 3" wide finished, they must be drawn 3 1/2" wide; two borders will use up 7" of your 45" width. After you draw in the top and bottom borders, 14" in width will be accounted for. All the other quilt pieces that will be cut from this particular fabric can be placed after the borders are drawn in place. A different cutting diagram is required for each of the fabrics that will be used in the quilt.

Most of the patterns in this section are given actual size. In some cases, a full-size piece would have been too big to fit on the pages, so a portion, usually a half, of the piece is given. You should use the portion to make your full-size pattern, then test the pattern by making a block. If the portion given is one-half the pattern, with a Place on the Fold line, that line is the center of the pattern piece. You can trace around half the pattern, then turn your paper so that the Place on the Fold lines are aligned, and trace the second half.

LONE STARS, BROKEN STARS, STARS OF BETHLEHEM AND SUNBURSTS

Shown on pages 18 through 39.

All of these designs are made from a 45-degree diamond, many different sizes of which are given on page 140. The lines on these stacked diamonds are spaced l/4" apart, so the cutting line for one diamond serves as the stitching line for the next size up. Measure one side of the diamond to find the size; do not measure from tip to tip. The diamond should be placed on the fabric so that the longest direction (through the center, from point to point) falls on the lengthwise grain of the fabric.

The first step is deciding on the number of diamonds that each of the eight big points will contain. It will need to have enough diamonds to accomodate all the colors you want to use. Diagram A contains four rows of four diamonds. You might want to make your pattern with six rows, or with ten rows. Adapt this diagram to your own design, keeping in mind that the diamonds do not have to be the same size in the diagram as they are in your pattern; this diagram is simply for your color scheme. When you

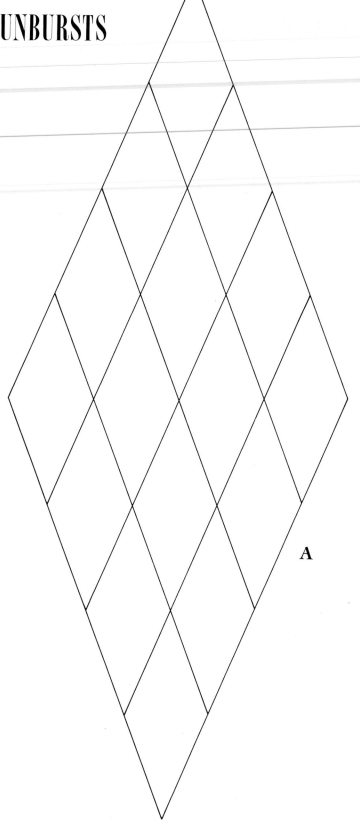

A

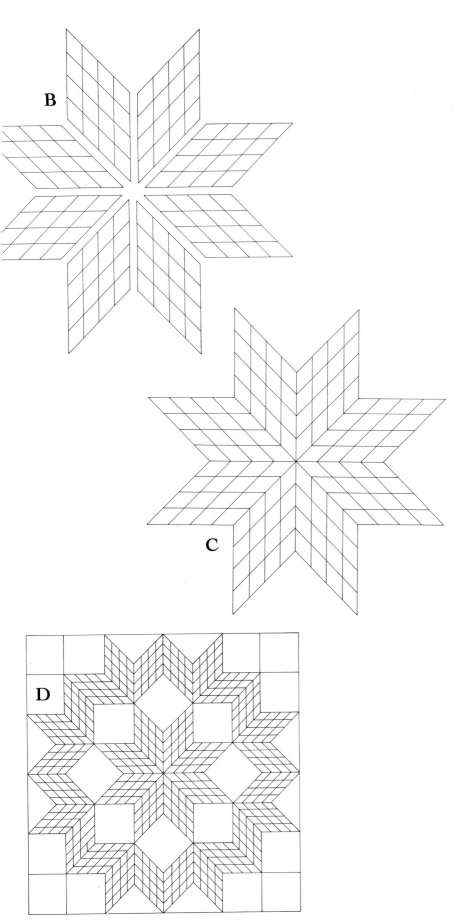

B

C

D

have decided on the number of diamonds you want in each row and the color placement, you will make eight large sections: see diagram B. Sew those sections together to make the Lone Star or Star of Bethlehem; see diagram C.

The Broken Star, diagram D, will require, in addition to the eight large pieced diamonds for the center star, twenty-four more pieced diamonds, which form the border around the star. Look at the examples on pages 28 to 31 for different color schemes.

The Lone Star and Star of Bethlehem are finished by the insertion of squares at the corners and triangles at the sides of the star. The size of these squares and triangles is determined by the length of the star points, and it is best to measure those points after they have been constructed.

The finishing of the Broken Star into a square is a bit more complicated. Study diagram D for necessary squares and triangles.

If you make a Sunburst, you will use only half of diagram A, which is a pieced triangle. Eight pieced triangles make each of the quilts on pages 38 to 39.

A SELECTION OF 45° DIAMONDS

Trace a diamond of the size needed from the selection given here. Sizes range from ⅝" to 6½". The lines are ¼" apart. Be sure to add a ¼" seam allowance to each diamond and to test the pattern before cutting your fabric.

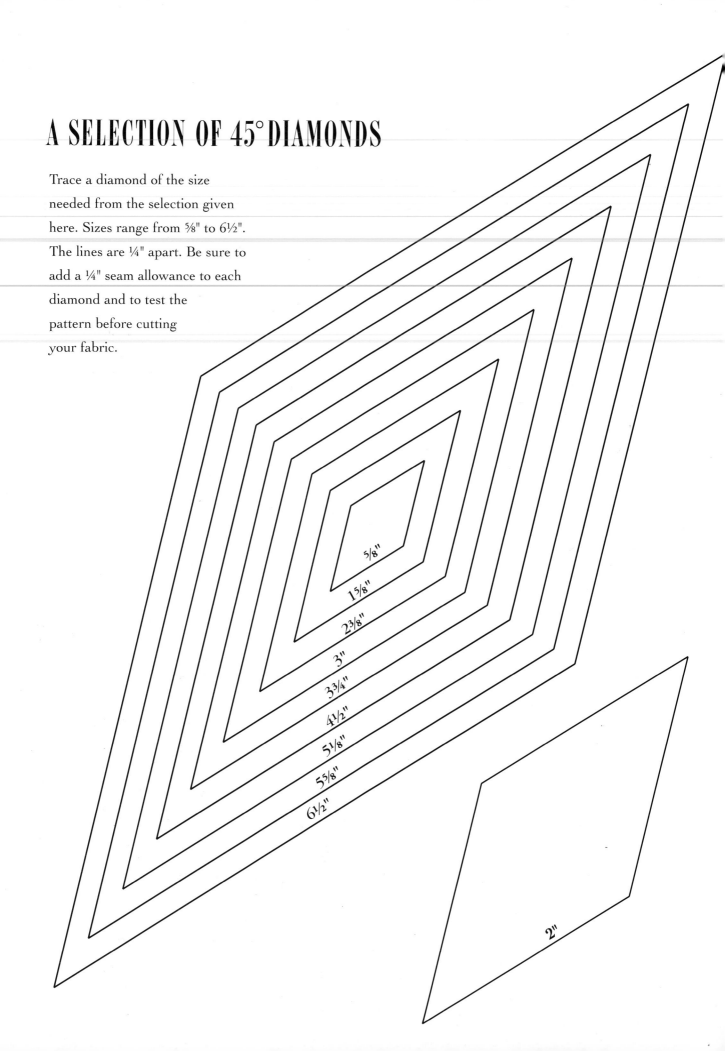

⅝"

1⅝"

2⅜"

3"

3¾"

4½"

5⅛"

5⅝"

6½"

2"

SIMPLE STAR OF LEMOYNE

Shown on page 96.

Size of finished block: 7" square

There are two ways to make the Star of LeMoyne, and it seems that the only difference between the two is personal choice. In one method, the diamonds are added to one another in a circular manner until the star is complete. In the other method, which is good if stripes are to be matched, the diamonds are sewn together into pairs, the pairs into halves, and the halves into a whole. The corner blocks and side triangles are added last.

All Stars of LeMoyne are made the same way, no matter what size they are. It is better, though, to hand piece the smaller stars. See "Hand Piecing the Eight-Point Star of LeMoyne," page 131. The bed-size Star of LeMoyne on pages 94 to 95, which also contains corner stars and half-stars, can be machine-pieced. To get a diamond large enough to make an entire quilt top, see The Super Star: Quilt Top in a Day, beginning on page 132.

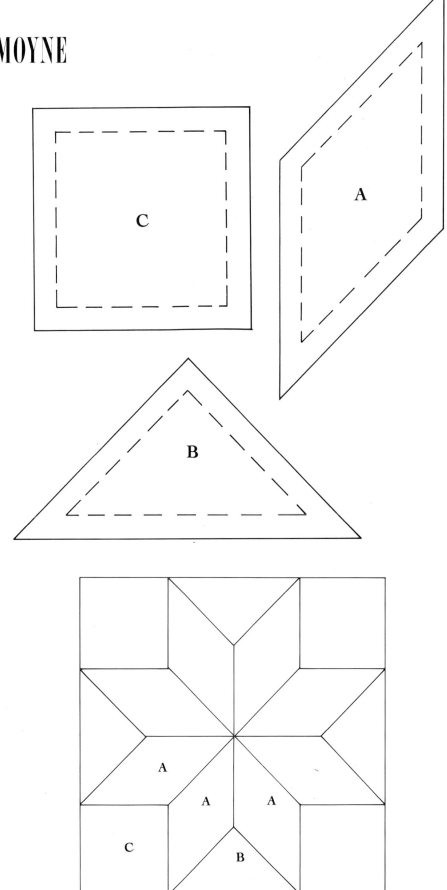

RADIANT STAR

Shown on page 46.

Size of finished block: 18" square

There are several ways that color can be manipulated in this design, especially with the center octagon and the surrounding triangles. In this example, the center octagon is much stronger than the surrounding triangles, but some variations feature a ring of small white triangles around the center octagon. This is one of the easiest of the Feathered Star patterns.

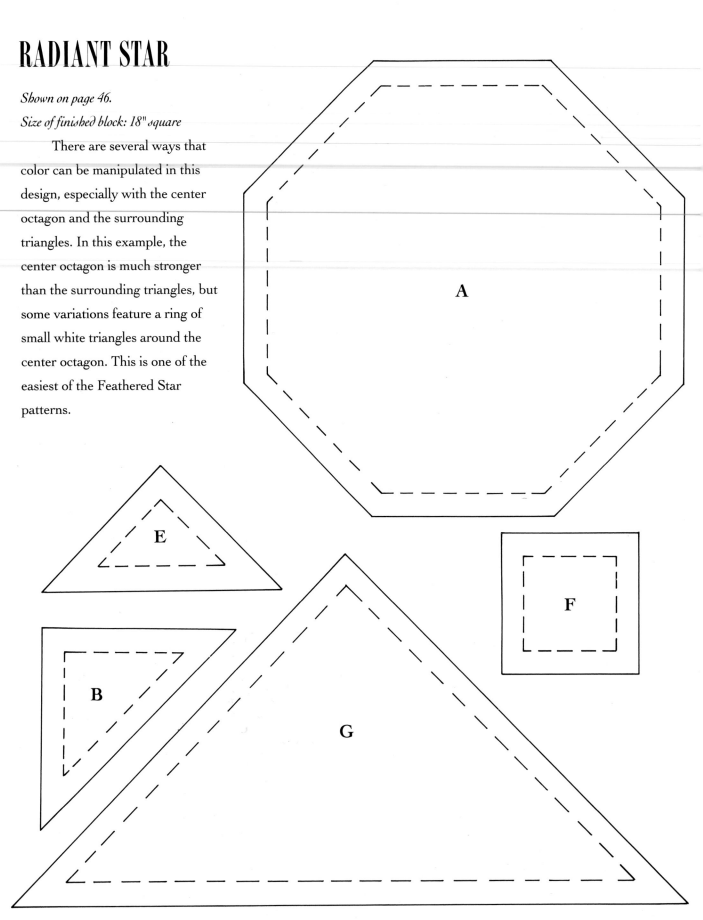

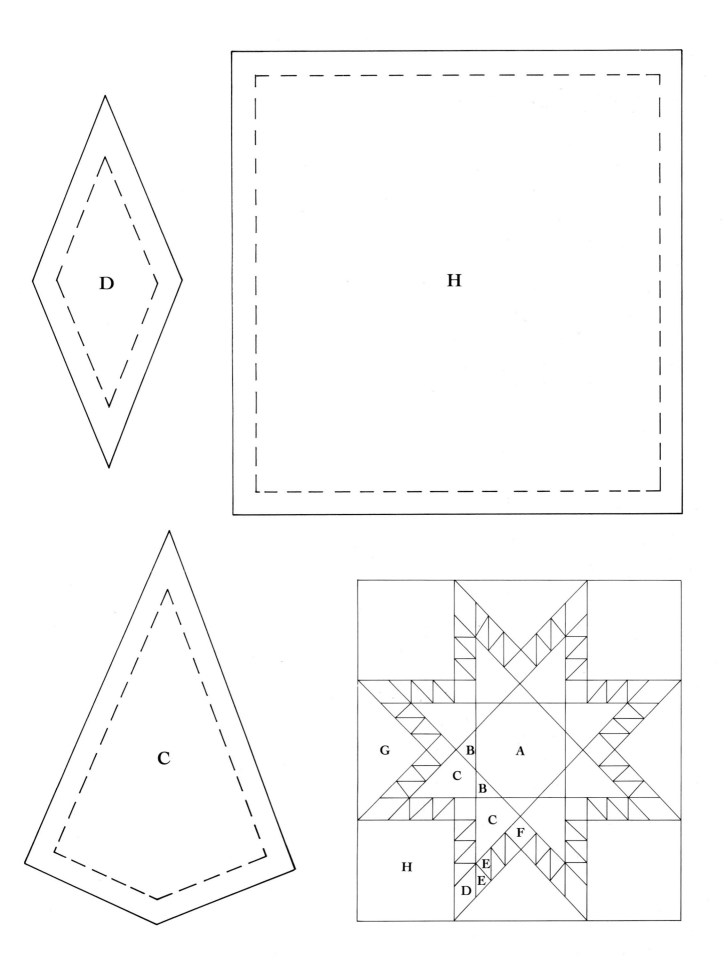

GROUPED OHIO STAR

Shown on page 51.

Size of finished block: 10" square

      Although the pieces required for just one block are numerous (there are 73 of them) and small, this quilt pattern can be accomplished with relative ease if the rotary cutter is used and speed piecing techniques are employed. Break the block down into rows to see how the piecing for each row should go. Piece an "E" section to either side of the "D" square so that you will be working with straight seams—you would not want to try to set the "D" square into the star points. If you plan to make the quilt as shown, be aware of the fact that the maker set the blocks on the diagonal.

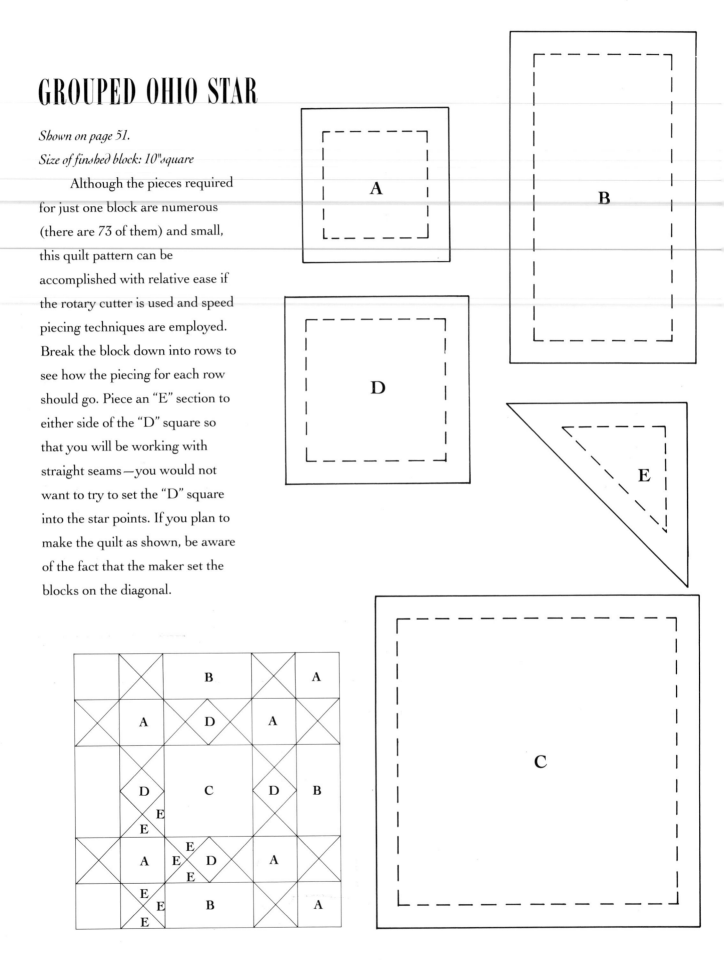

BETANCOURT STAR

Shown on page 53.

Size of finished block: 11 1/4" square

This star will make up
quickly, especially if you follow
the Unit Method of Construction
as explained on pages 120 to 121.
The use of unpatterned blocks
between the patterned ones means
that the quilt top goes together
fairly quickly; those plain blocks
will have to be beautifully quilted,
though, if your quilt is to be as
lovely as this one.

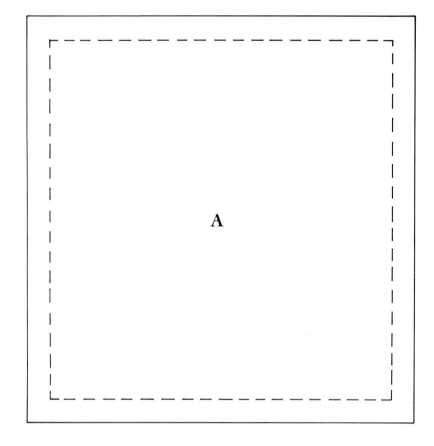

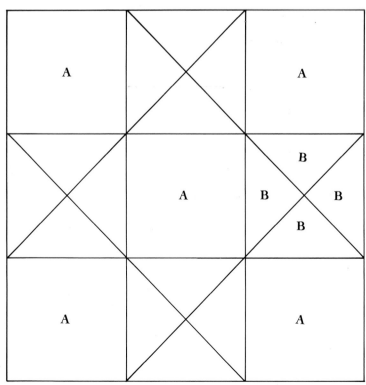

OHIO STAR, OHIO STAR

Shown on page 54.

Size of finished block: 9" square

    Patti O'Connor, the designer of this quilt, has provided easy-to-follow schematics for color placement that unlock the secret to this quilt's puzzle. Since the sewing is not difficult, this quilt is fun to make, and is a most innovative way to make use of scraps.

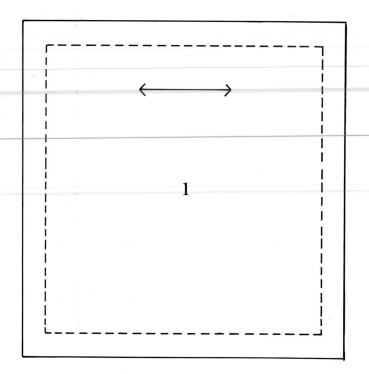

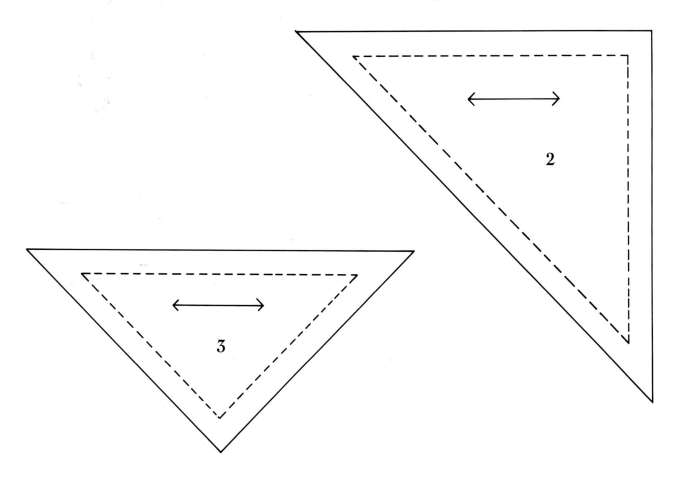

Block Diagrams

Block C

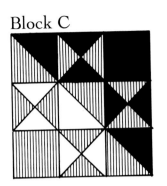

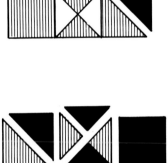

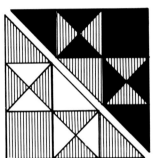

Block D

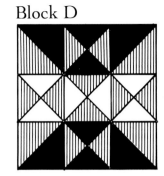

Block A

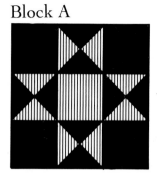

Block B

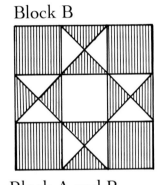

Block A and B

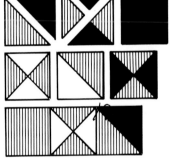

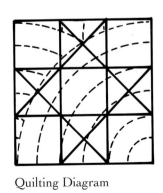

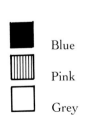

Blue

Pink

Grey

Quilting Diagram

Top Assembly Diagram

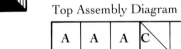

A	A	A	C	A		C	A	A	A
A	A	A	B	D		B	A	A	A
A	A	A	C	A		C	A	A	A
C	B		C	B	B	B	C	B	C
A	D		A	B	B	B	A	D	A
C		B	C	B	B	B		C	B	C
A	A	A	C	A		C	A	A	A
A	A	A	B	D		B	A	A	A
A	A	A	C		A	C	A	A	A

STARRY EVENING

Shown on page 55.

Size of finished block: 15" square

Although we give a piecing diagram for the star design so that you can sew up a test block, the best way to put this quilt together is to do it in strips, as illustrated on page 150. This is an example of a design in which the overall design of the quilt is carried in the sashing (those strips inserted between blocks). Actually, the blocks are plain, and the sashing is pieced. You will find it helpful to trace the illustrations for setting the rows together and color the pieces according to your own scheme.

A

PLACE ON FOLD

F

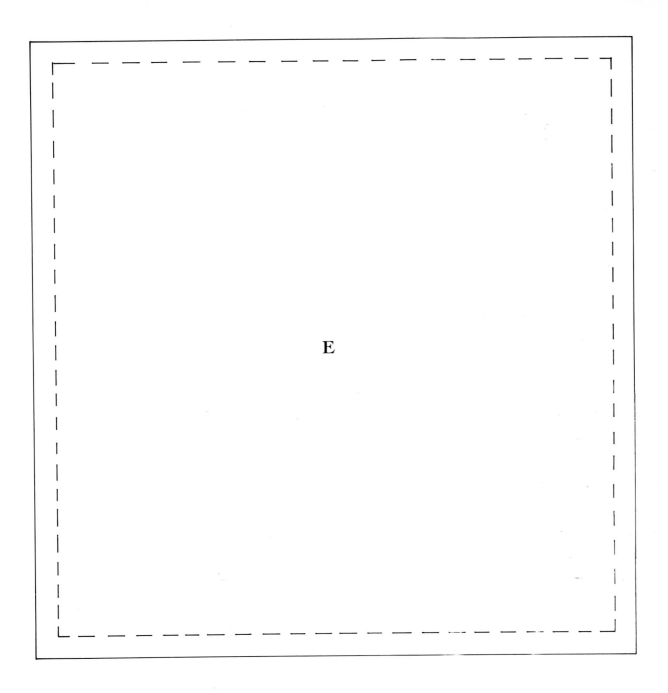

E

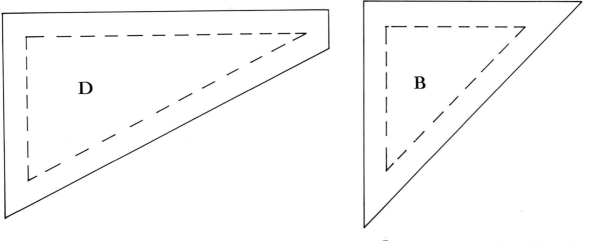

D

B

CONTINUED ON NEXT PAGE

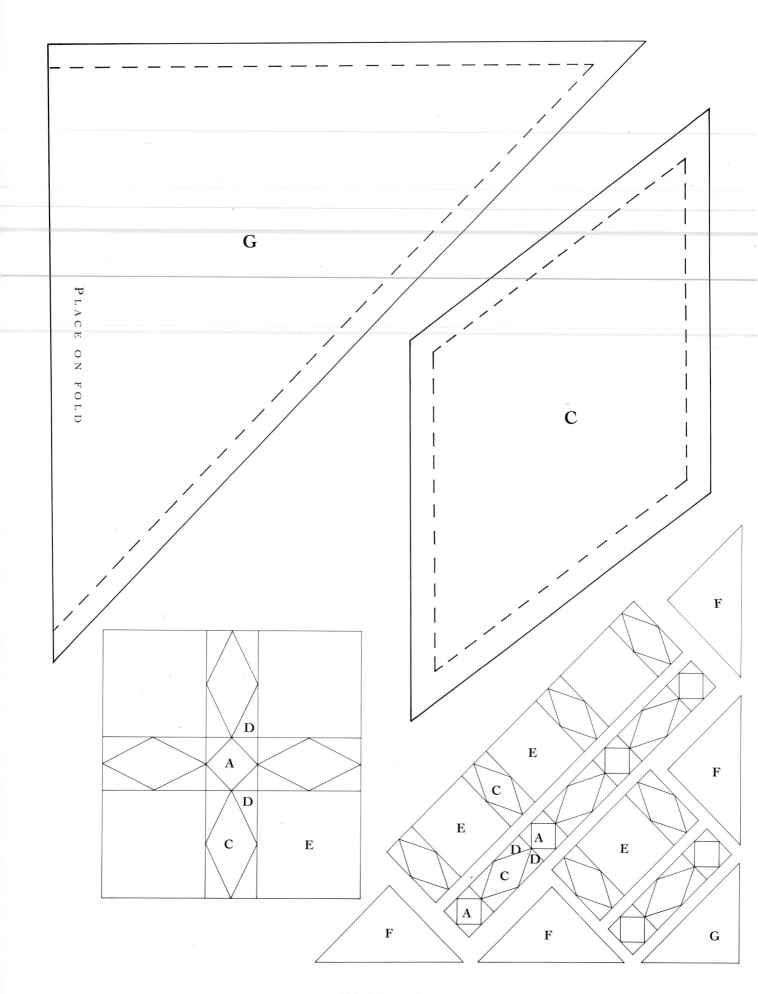

G

PINK STARS AND HEXAGONS TUMBLING BLOCKS

Shown on pages 62 to 63.

Size of finished block: pink star is 9 1/4" from tip to tip; star in Tumbling Blocks is 4 1/2".

The best way to put this quilt together is to piece all the hexagons and all the stars, then sew a hexagon onto two opposite sides of every star. When two star/hexagon units are fitted to one another, they form the beginning of a long diagonal row, which will run from the lower left corner to the upper right corner of the quilt. Make subsequent rows by adding star/hexagon units to either side of the long row, making each row shorter by one star. Study the photograph of Tumbling Blocks on page 63 to accurately position the tri-colored hexagons to make vertical chains of diamonds.

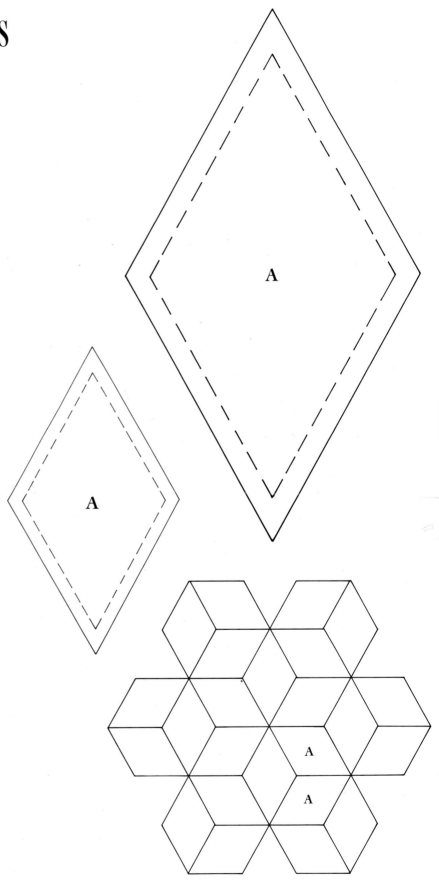

ROLLING STAR

Shown on pages 104 to 105.

Size of finished block: 14 1/2" square

Before beginning a Rolling Star, you should carefully study our examples to see the different effects that color placement produces. If the squares between the blocks are all the same color, as on page 105, a rolling effect is obtained. If the squares are of different colors, and if they match the outer ring of diamonds, the star seems to swirl (page 104).

It is best to piece the center star, then add the squares all around. Fit the outer row of diamonds in between the squares, and, finally, add the corner triangles. The design is easy to hand piece, and the work goes quickly.

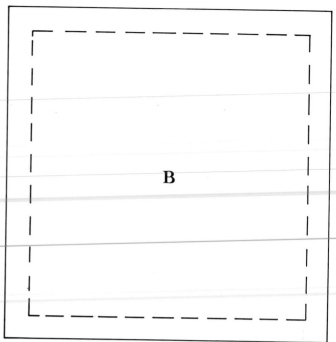

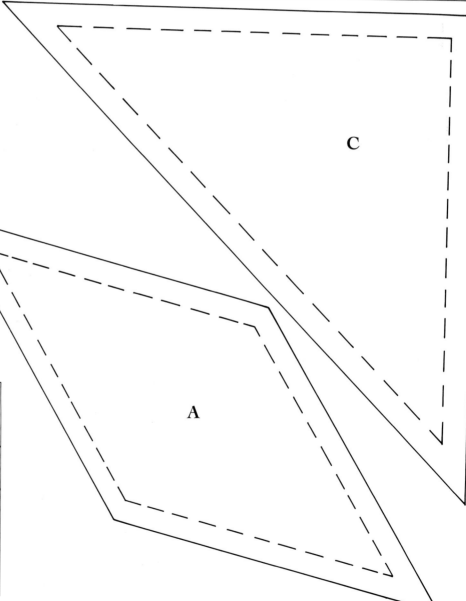

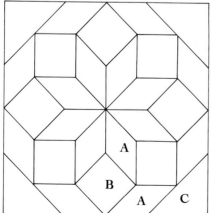

KALEIDOSCOPE OR WINDMILL STAR

Shown on pages 66 to 67.

Size of finished block: each star unit is 7 5/8" square.

Despite the complex look of this quilt, it does not take a lot of time to make. The star unit is made in two different color schemes, set together in panels. In both color schemes, the star points are two different colors, and they are set into a striped background square. It is choice of fabrics that makes the two blocks so different and so interesting.

The piecing can easily be done on the sewing machine. The quilt as shown is fairly small (69 1/2" x 72 1/2"), but it can be enlarged simply by adding rows within the panels, if the color scheme permits, or by adding panels. Of course, increasing the length is simply a matter of adding more star blocks to the top or bottom. However, the secondary pattern in the side panels is formed when four blocks are put together, so the length would have to be increased by four blocks if the pattern were to be preserved.

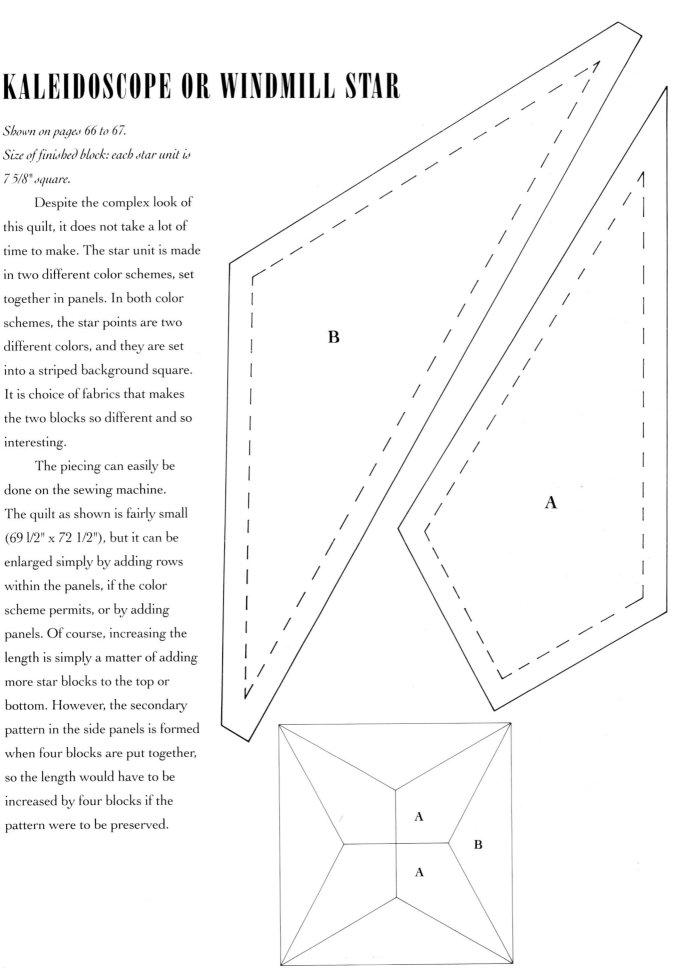

HARBOR LIGHTS

Shown on pages 68 to 69.

Size of finished block: 11" square

    The points of the star are made up of four triangles of the same size; they must, of course, be put together first. The star points can then be sewn to the center square; the last step is the fitting into place of the "C" triangles.

    This quilt can be machine-pieced.

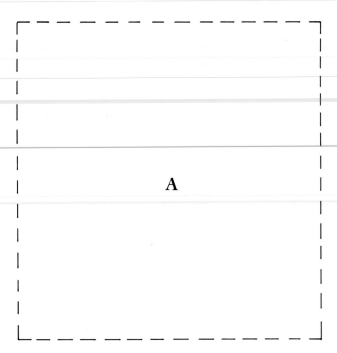

A

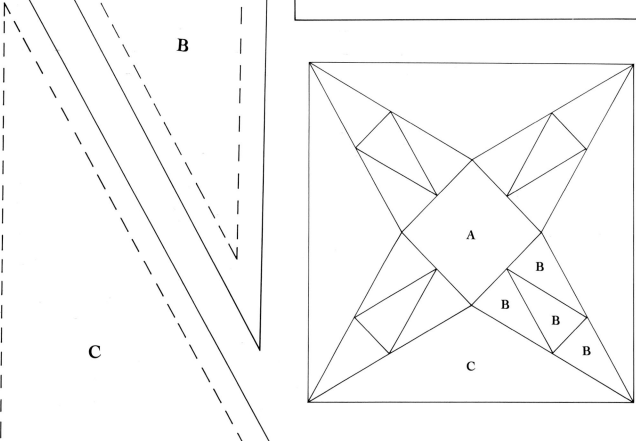

B

C

PLACE ON FOLD

PINE BURR

Shown on pages 70 to 71.
Size of finished block: star is 15 3/4"
from tip to tip.

    The star points must be put
together first, then joined to the
central square. The large black
diamonds and half diamonds that
join the stars and finish the
quilt are put in after
the stars are made.

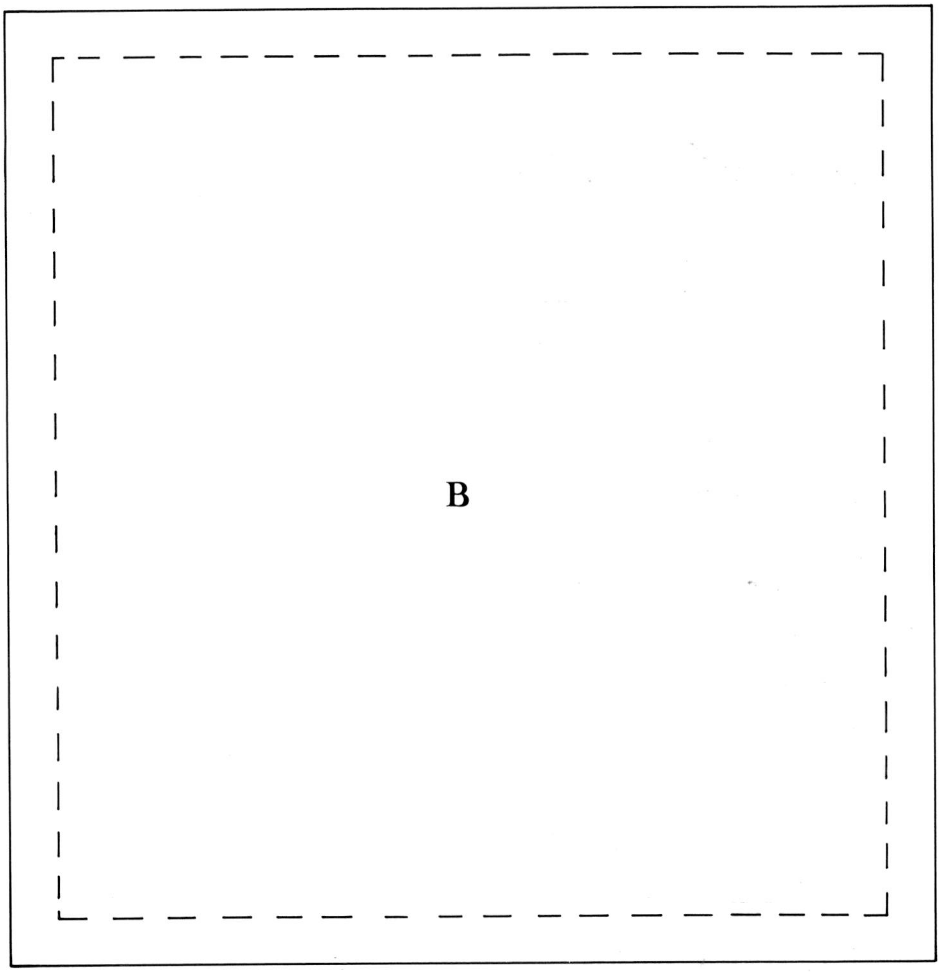

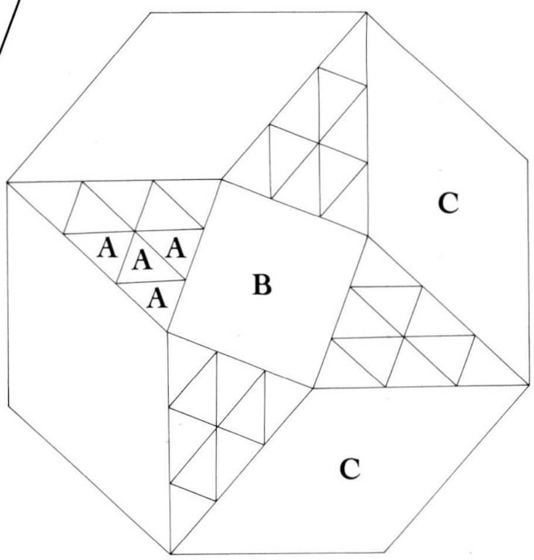

B

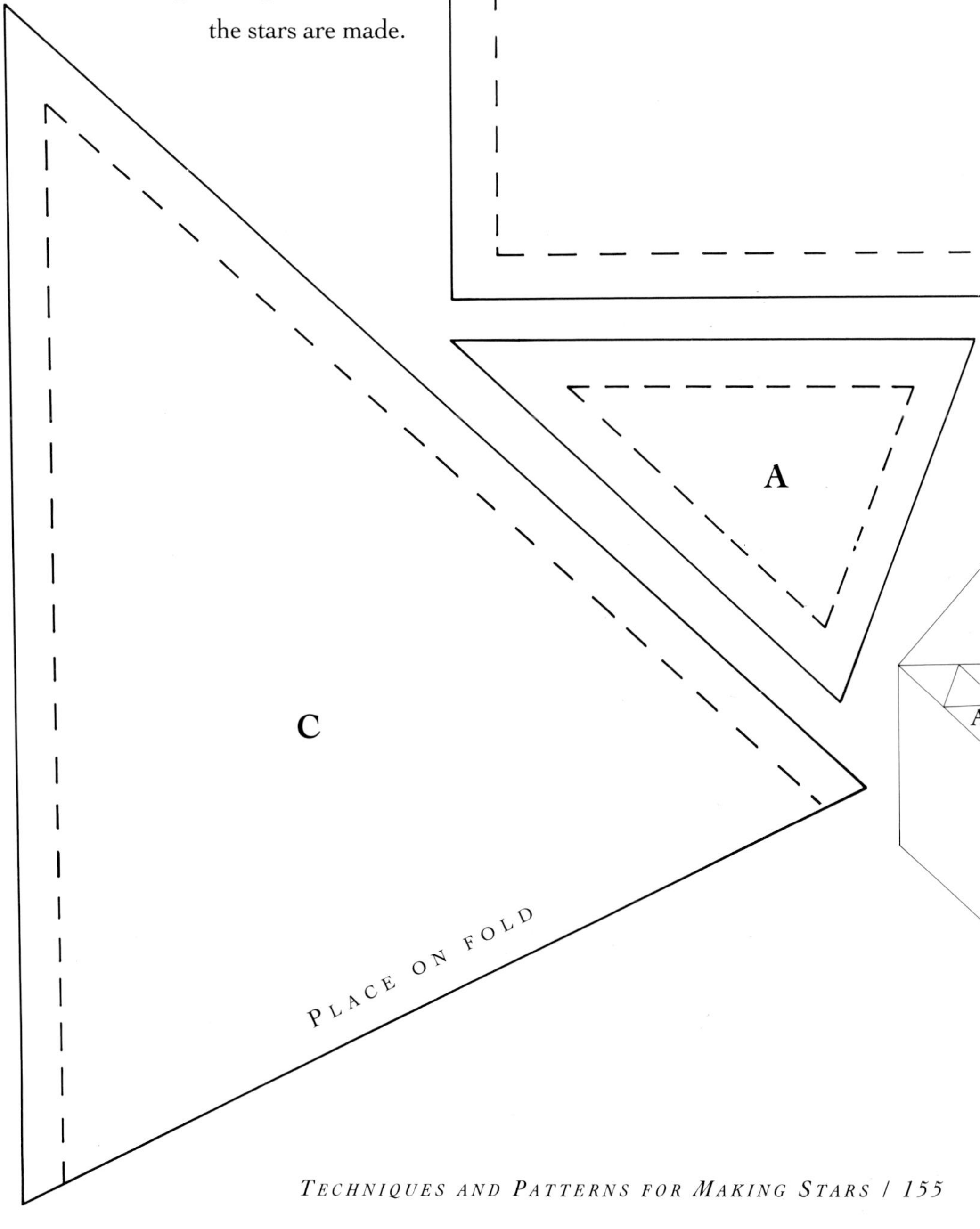

A

C

PLACE ON FOLD

TEXAS STAR

Shown on page 74.

Size of finished block: circle is 8 3/4",
block is 14" square

As in the two preceding patterns, the best way to work this star is to proceed from the center out. Sew the star points to the pentagon, then insert the wedges between the star points. The resulting circle can then be appliquéd onto a background square, or it can be set into the square if the circle is traced onto the background and cut away. Remember to allow for a seam, if you follow this second, more difficult way.

The sashing strips between the blocks are 1 1/2" wide, both vertically and horizontally, but the side borders are 3 1/4" wide, while the top and bottom ones are only 1" on this old quilt.

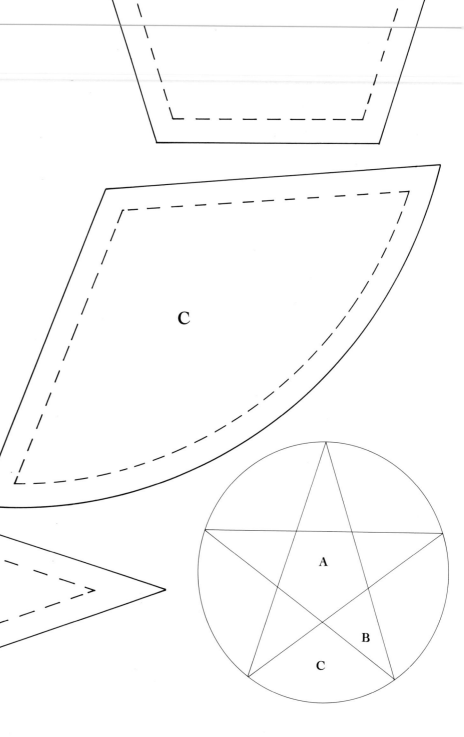

A

C

B

A

B

C

SMOOTHING IRON

Shown on page 77.
Size of finished block: each leg of the triangle is 6 1/2".

The construction of this quilt pattern is fascinating because it is so unusual; the building block of the quilt is a tiny triangle bordered with strips and diamonds. When those triangles are set together in strips, one up and one down, white stars are formed.

The sequence for stitching does not seem to be the most logical, until you realize that it keeps you from having awkward joinings. First, sew a strip "B" to one side of the "C" triangle. Next, sew an "A" diamond to one end of a "B" strip, and "A" diamonds to both ends of another "B" strip. Sew the strip with one diamond to the "CB" unit, matching the seam of the strip to the seam of the "CB" unit. You will now have a "C" triangle that is bordered on two sides with a diamond at the junction of the borders. Sew the remaining strip, with the two diamonds, in place, and the triangle will be complete.

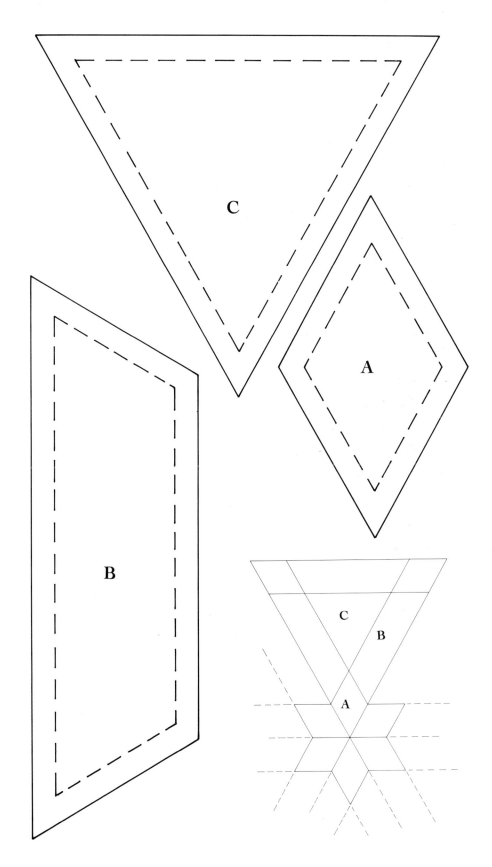

MARINER'S COMPASS

Shown on page 83.

Size of finished block: circle is 14" in diameter; block is 18" square.

In a Mariner's Compass such as this one, in which the rays are bi-color, in light and dark fabrics, construction is much faster with the use of a shortcut technique. First, sew light and dark strips of fabric together; the strips should be as wide as the widest part of the pattern piece for the ray. Then, lay the pattern on the sewn strip with the straight seam line of the pattern exactly on the seam of the strip and trace the outside edge of the pattern onto the strip. (You might want to make a template from the pattern that is the same size as the finished ray.) When you cut on the traced lines, the entire ray is cut, sewn, and ready for use. It is much easier to make the rays this way than by cutting out each half of the ray and then sewing them together. In this particular Mariner's Compass, this method is the best for the "B" and "C" rays; do not use it for the "A" rays; you will see why when the piecing sequence is explained.

Once the rays are made, the piecing sequence begins. You will

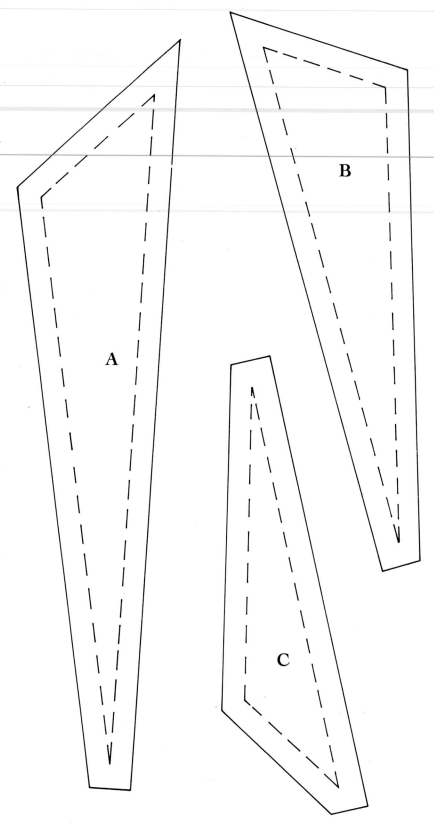

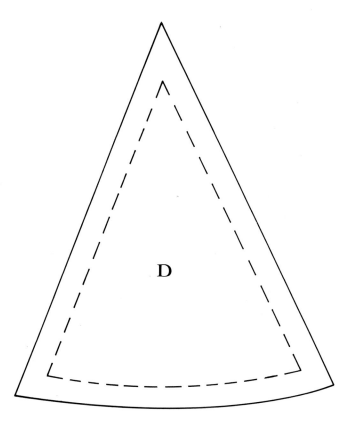

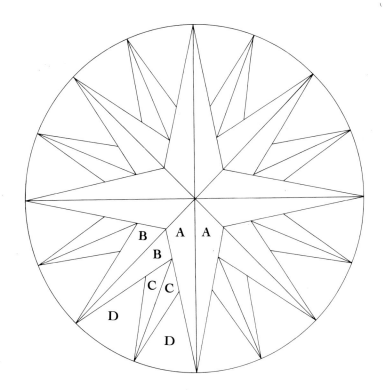

work in quadrants of the circle, or one-fourth at a time. First, piece a "D" section to either side of a complete "C" ray. Do this twice, because there are two "C" rays in each quadrant. Next, sew one of these "CD" sections to either side of the "B" ray. Complete these steps for all four of the quadrants.

To complete the Mariner's Compass, sew a half of the "A" ray onto either side of the "BCD" wedges, always sewing the light half to the right side of the wedge and the dark half to the left side of the wedge. Sew two of the completed quadrants together to make half the circle, then sew the two halves together.

The completed Mariner's Compass can either be appliquéd onto or set into a background square. If you appliqué it in place, which is easier, you should cut away the fabric beneath the Compass after the appliqué is complete to eliminate bulk.

(*NOTE:* An excellent source for constructing the Mariner's Compass and for additional patterns is Judy Mathieson's *Mariner's Compass: An American Quilt Classic,* from C & T Publishing, P.O. Box 1456, Layfayette, CA 94549.)

SEVEN DANCING SISTERS

Shown on pages 86 to 87.

Size of finished block: 17 1/4" square

This is a unique variation on a pattern that is unusual to begin with — any quilt in the Seven Sisters pattern is a treasure, but I have only seen one example of this design. Be sure to study the color photograph to see how a secondary pattern emerges when the pentagons are all made in the same color.

One who is skilled in piecing might devise a plan that would involve sewing the "B" triangles to the "C" pentagons, which would eliminate the tedious business of piecing inside corners. However, for those who are easily confused, the best route to follow is to piece the star points "B" onto the star centers "A", then set the stars together with the pentagons "C". Finish the star section into a circle with the addition of sections "D". Although the pattern is given for piece "E" to finish the circle into a square, the easier way is to applique the star circle onto a background square that measures 17 1/4", then cut away the background fabric underneath the circle.

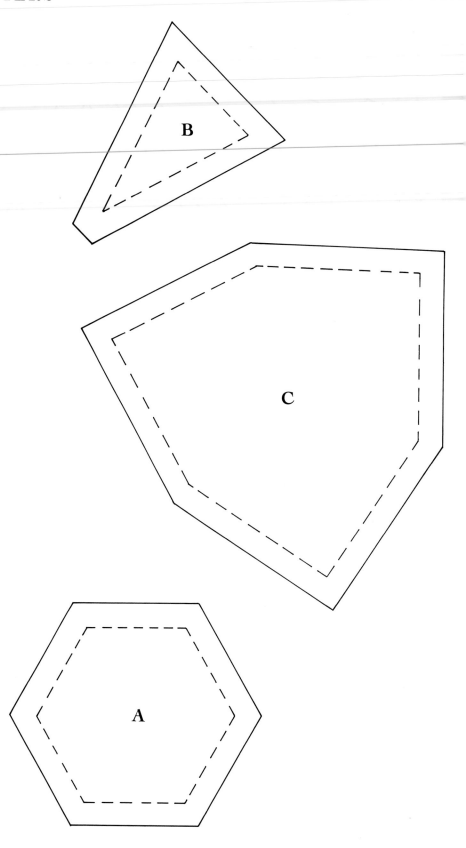

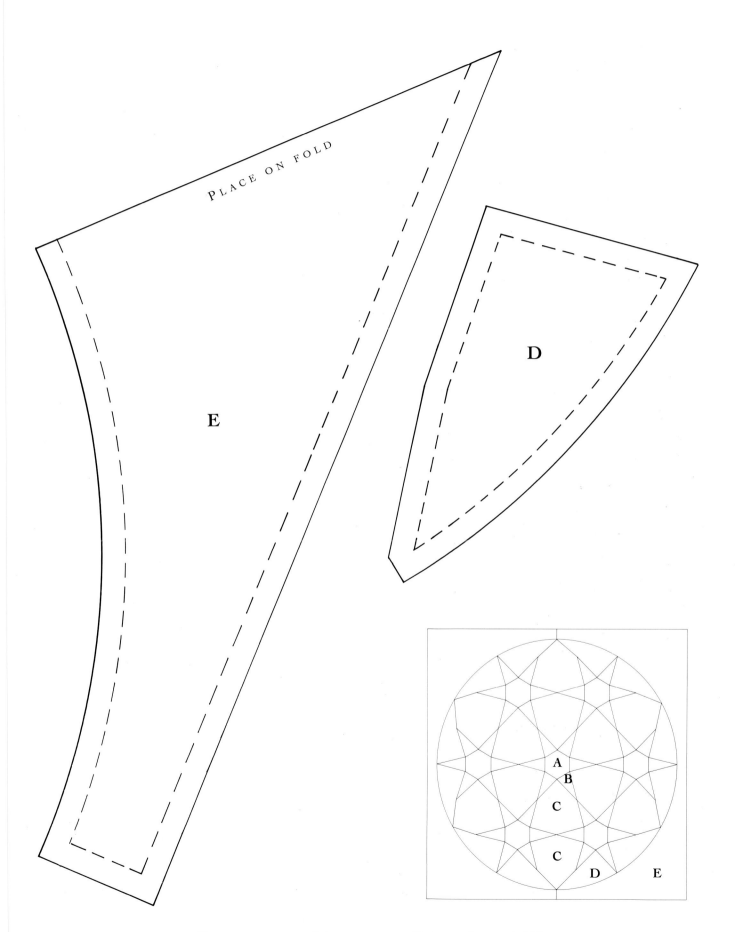

PLACE ON FOLD

E

D

A
B
C
C
D
E

TOUCHING STARS

Shown on page 100. Size of block: each star is 11" from tip to tip; the larger setting block is 6" square.

In this example of Touching Stars, the pattern is set on the diagonal, always a good way to add interest to a quilt. The best way of working is to piece the stars first from the "A" diamonds, then fill in at the points of the stars with the "B" squares. Add the "C" squares last.

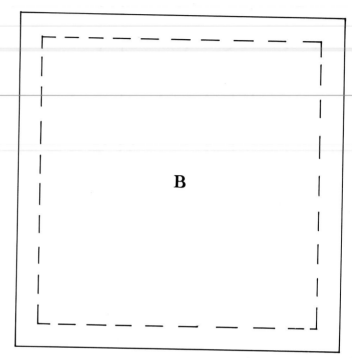

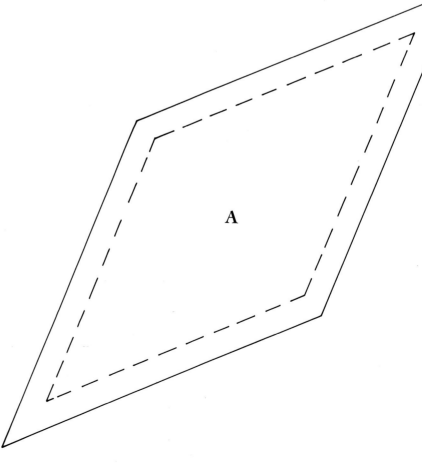

S

Sh
blo

cen
Car
dia
the
star
bet
sm
ma
are
and
the
half
cor

C

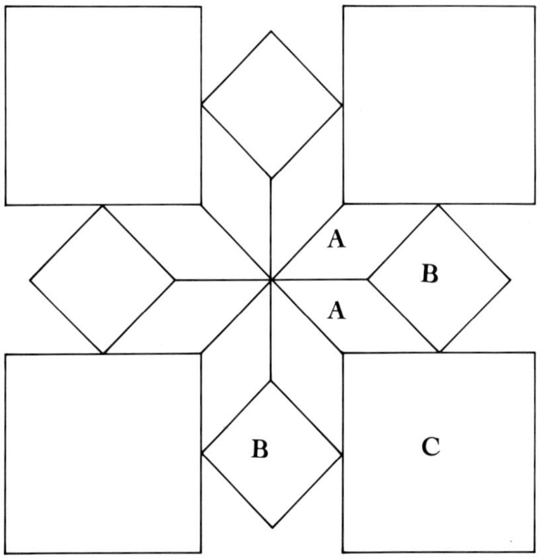

A
B
A
B
C

STARRY PATHS

Shown on the frontispiece (opposite the title page). Size of finished block: 8" square.

When the blocks are set next to one another, as shown in the photograph, the sparkling energy of Starry Paths blends all the stars into a single design. Yet, the stars still twinkle merrily when the blocks are separated by sashing, if you choose to use it.

This design has endless color possiblities. Plan out your color scheme carefully before cutting. In the photograph, the smaller triangles, C, are cut from the same white-dotted orange fabric. The long rays, A, are cut from such a wide variety of fabrics that it seems at first that none is repeated. In some color schemes, only two fabrics are used for the long rays, and two for the short ones.

This star goes together a little differently from designs you may be accustomed to. If you run an imaginary diagonal line across the center of the block, from corner to corner, you will see that the two halves are mirror images. When you follow my piecing sequence, you will put together the two halves, then join them on that diagonal seam. And, you will already have the background in place!

To piece the star, first sew a B and a D (both are background pieces)

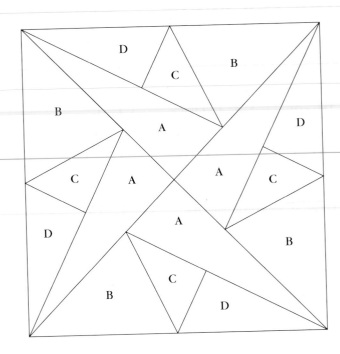

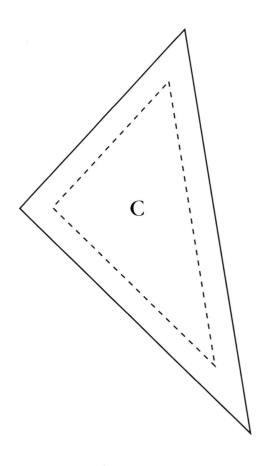

to a C. Then sew the BCD section to an A. Repeat, then sew an AB section to the free side of A to make half the star. Repeat for the other half of the star. Sew the two halves together in a diagonal seam across the center to complete the design.

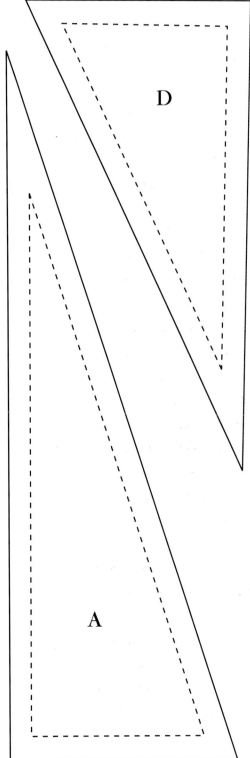

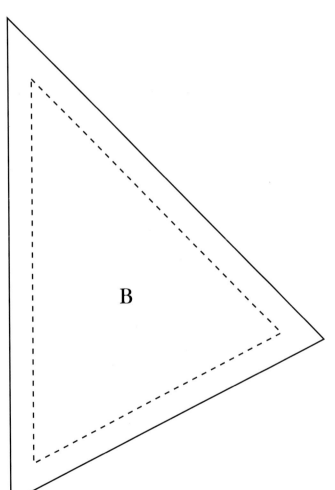

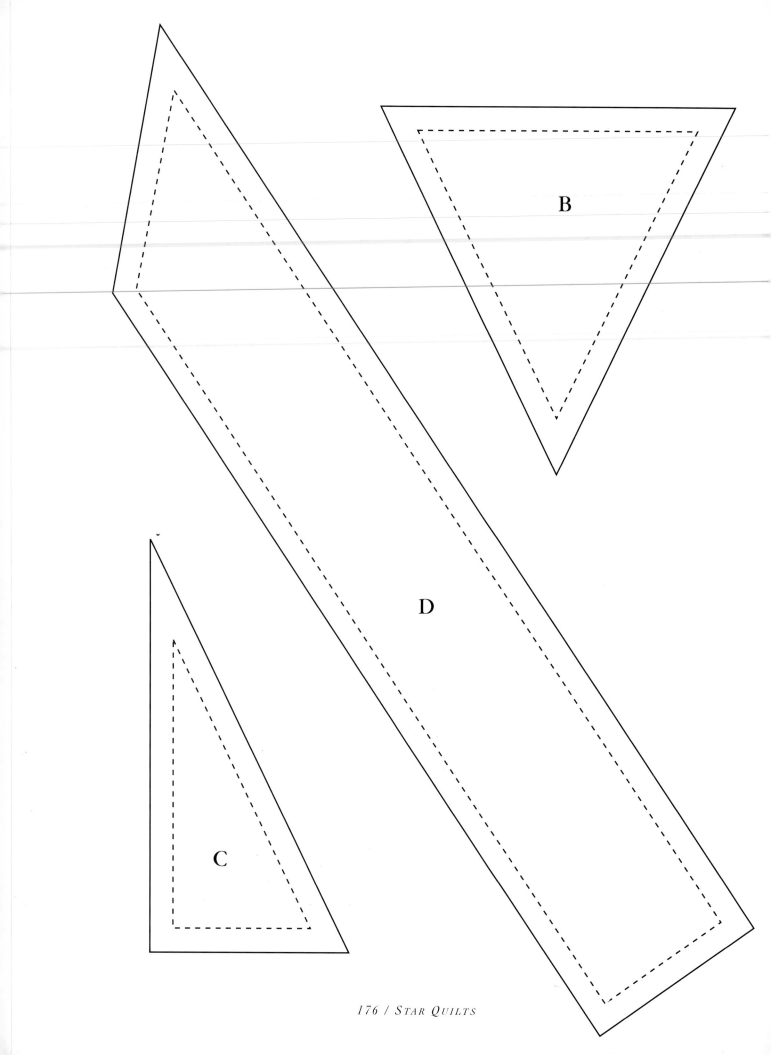

B

D

C

AUTOGRAPH STAR

Shown on page 76.

Size of finished block: The finished star measures approximately 8⅔" across the center from point to point. Each connecting diamond is approximately 4⅓" long.

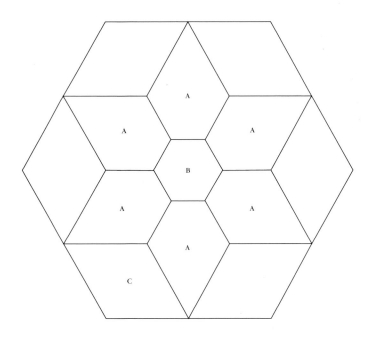

Though it looks simple, this daisy-like pattern is very exacting to piece. There are two methods of construction: the first conventional, and the second a rather unusual technique that eliminates six inside corners. Choose the one you feel most comfortable with, or try both and see which works best for you.

In the conventional method, sew the six points of the star together, then set the center hexagon into the opening. It is possible to machine-stitch the points together, but the hexagon must be stitched carefully in place by hand so that each of its corners can be exactly matched to a seam.

The alternative method forms a more exact hexagon and is done by machine. The points opposite each other are stitched to the hexagon in pairs, one point at a time. Stitch a point onto the hexagon (leaving the side seam allowances of the point free). Then attach the point directly across the hexagon. Continue to work in pairs like this until all six points are stitched onto the hexagon, like loose

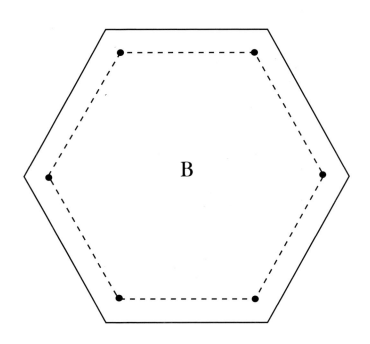

petals. The side seams of the points are sewn to one another only after all are attached to the hexagon.

No matter which method you use, you will find it best to make up all your stars first, then set them together with the white diamonds. For best results, hand piece.

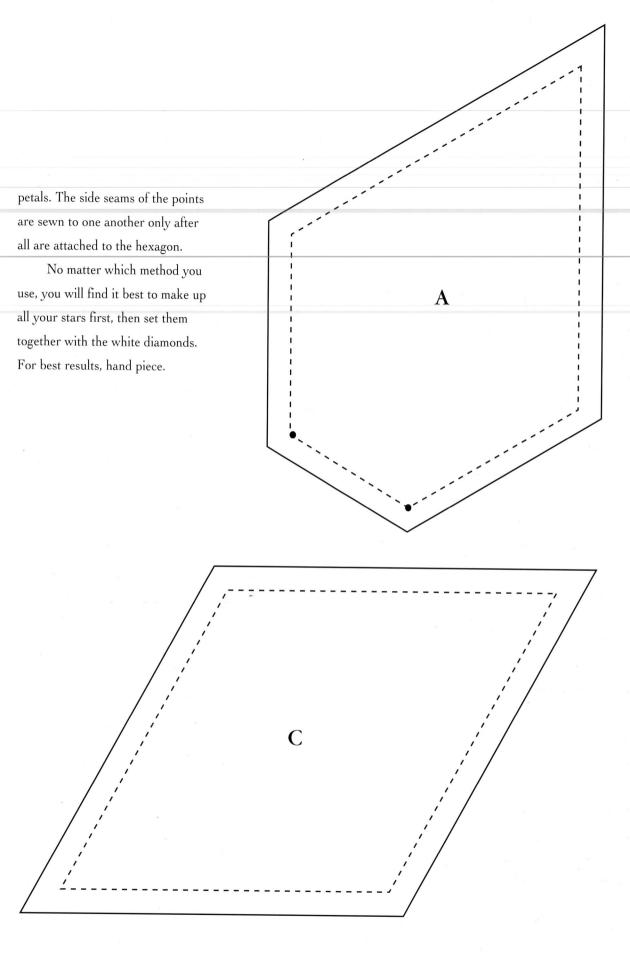

A

C

MARINER'S COMPASS WITH CENTER CIRCLE

Shown on page 83.
Size of finished block: 36" square.

Slightly more difficult to piece than Mariner's Compass, described on page 158, because of the center circle, this pattern uses many of the same techniques. Work from outside toward the center, completing one-fourth of the design at a time.

Sew an A piece to either side of a B piece. Repeat four times for one quadrant of the design. Attach an AB section to either side of a C ray, to make two ABC sections. Sew the ABC sections to either side of a D piece. Make four of these quadrants, then sew them to either side of the large E points to complete the circular design.

Carefully slipstitch piece F in place over the opening at the center of the compass, smoothly turning under the seam allowance to make a perfect circle. Stitch corner sections G in place to complete the block. Note that only half of piece G is given; place on a fold as indicated to obtain a full-size piece. Alternatively, the complete Mariner's Compass can be appliquéed to a background square of fabric.

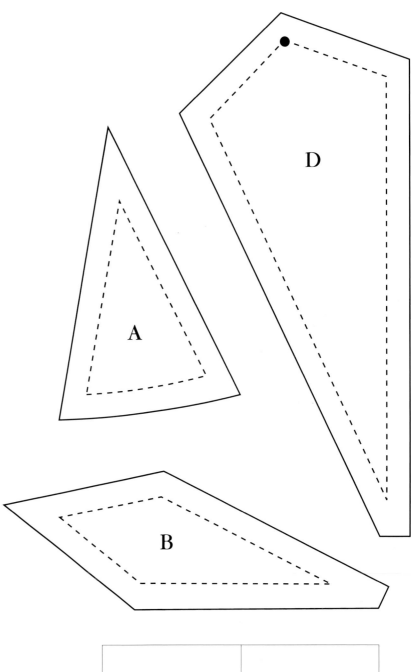

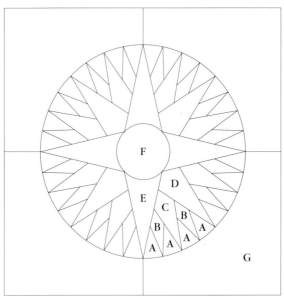

FLYING SWALLOWS

Shown on page 107.

Size of finished block: 12" square.

This beautiful star is a pleasure
for those who love working with color.
One of the most effective schemes I've
seen has the swallows in black, set
into a yellow diamond. The fill-in
squares and triangles are in a tiny
black-and-white print. Some clever
quilters have given an entirely different twist to the design for Christmas
by making the swallows in green and
using a combination of red, white, and
red-and-white prints to finish it. The
green diamonds take on the appearance of a wreath.

Because the pieces are so small,
hand piecing works best. Put together
three A pieces, then fill in with B to
complete one pieced diamond.
Continue in this manner until eight
diamonds are finished. Then sew the
diamonds together and fill in with the
D corner squares and the C triangles.

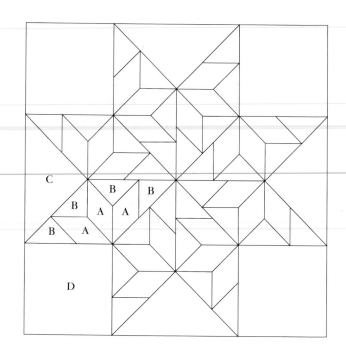

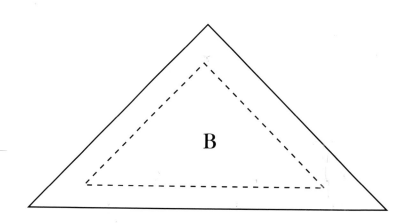

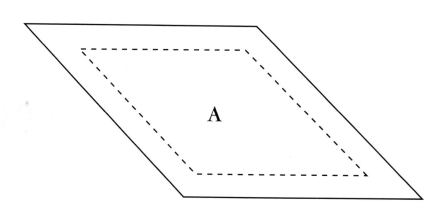

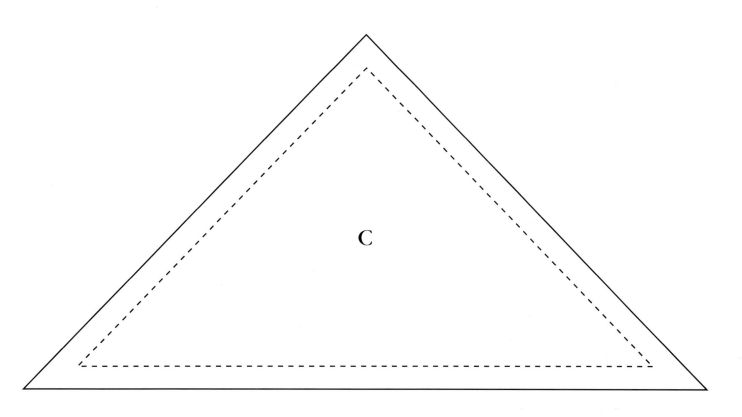

C

D

PROVENANCE OF QUILTS

BIBLIOGRAPHY AND SELECTED READING

Beyer, Jinny. *Patchwork Patterns*. McLean, VA: EPM Publications, Inc., 1979.

Beyer, Jinny. *The Scrap Look*. McLean, VA: EPM Publications, Inc., 1985.

Binney, 3d, Edwin and Binney-Winslow, Gail. *Homage to Amanda: Two Hundred Years of American Quilts*. San Francisco: R K Press, 1984.

Bishop, Robert; Secord, William; and Weissman, Judith Reiter. *Quilts, Coverlets, Rugs, and Samplers*. New York: Alfred A. Knopf, Chanticleer Press, 1982.

Brackman, Barbara. *An Encyclopedia of Pieced Quilt Patterns, Revised, Volumes 1 through 8*. Lawrence, KS: Prairie Flower Publishing, 1984.

Brackman, Barbara. *Clues in the Calico: A Guide to Identifying and Dating Antique Quilts*. McLean, VA: EPM Publications, 1989.

Breshenhan, Karoline Patterson, and Puentes, Nancy O'Bryant. *Lone Stars: A Legacy of Texas Quilts, 1836–1936*. Austin: University of Texas Press, 1986.

Bullard, Lacy Folmar and Shiell, Betty Jo. *Chintz Quilts: Unfading Glory*. Tallahassee: Serendipity Publishers, 1983.

Burner, David, et al. *An American Portrait: A History of the United States*. New York: Charles Scribner's Sons, 1985.

Cargo, Robert T. "Long Remembered: An Alabama Pioneer and Her Quilts," *The Quilt Digest, Volume 3*. San Francisco: The Quilt Digest Press, 1986, 60–69.

Clarke, Mary Washington. *Kentucky Quilts and Their Makers*. Lexington: The University Press of Kentucky, 1976.

Cooper, Patricia and Buferd, Norma Bradley. *The Quilters: Women and Domestic Art*. Garden City, NY: Doubleday & Company, Inc., 1977.

DeGraw, Imelda. *The Denver Art Museum Quilts and Coverlets*. Denver: The Denver Art Museum, 1974.

DuBois, Jean. *A Galaxy of Stars: America's Favorite Quilts*. Durango, CO: La Plata Press, 1976.

Duke, Dennis and Harding, Deborah, eds. *America's Glorious Quilts*. New York: Hugh Lauter Levin Associates, Inc., 1987.

Ferraro, Pat; Hedges, Elaine; and Silber, Julie. *Hearts and Hands: The Influence of Women and Quilts on American Society*. San Francisco: The Quilt Digest Press, 1987.

Finley, Ruth E. *Old Patchwork Quilts and the Women Who Made Them*. Philadelphia: J.B. Lippincott & Co., 1929.

Fisher, Laura. *Quilts of Illusion*. Pittstown, NJ: The Main Street Press, 1988.

Fox, Sandi. *Small Endearments: Nineteenth-Century Quilts for Children*. New York: Charles Scribner's Sons, 1985.

Gross, Joyce. *A Patch in Time*. Catalog from an exhibit sponsored by the Mill Valley Quilt Authority, 1973.

Hall, Carrie A. and Kretsinger, Rose G. *The Romance of the Patchwork Quilt in America*. Caldwell, ID: Caxton Printers Ltd., Bonanza Books, 1935.

Holstein, Jonathan. *The Pieced Quilt: An American Design Tradition*. Boston: New York Graphic Society, 1973.

Ickis, Marguerite. *The Standard Book of Quilt Making and Collecting*. New York: Greystone Press, 1949.

Irwin, John Rice. *A People and Their Quilts*. Exton, PA: Schiffer Publishing Ltd., 1984.

Johnson, Mary Elizabeth. *Prize Country Quilts*. Birmingham: Oxmoor House, Inc., 1977.

The Kentucky Quilt Project. *Kentucky Quilts: 1800–1900*. Louisville, KY: Time Capsules: The Kentucky Quilt Project, 1982.

Khin, Yvonne M. *The Collector's Dictionary of Quilt Names and Patterns*. Washington, D.C.: Acropolis Books, Ltd., 1980.

Kile, Michael, ed. *The Quilt Digest, Volumes 3 and 4*. San Francisco: The Quilt Digest Press, 1985–1986.

Kiracofe, Roderick and Kile, Michael, eds. *The Quilt Digest, Volumes 1 and 2*. San Francisco: Kiracofe and Kile, 1983–1984.

LaBranche, Carol. *A Constellation for Quilters*. Pittstown, NJ: The Main Street Press, 1986.

Lasansky, Jeannette. *Pieced by Mother: Over 100 Years of Quiltmaking Traditions*, 1987. *Pieced by Mother: Symposium Papers*, 1988. *In the Heart of Pennsylvania: 19th and 20th Century Quiltmaking Traditions*, 1985. *In the Heart of Pennsylvania: Symposium Papers*, 1986. (All of the above published by the Oral Traditions Project of the Union County Courthouse, Lewisburg, Pennsylvania.)

Leman, Bonnie, ed. *Quilter's Newsletter Magazine*. Wheatridge, CO: Leman Publications, Inc., 1969-present.

Leon, Eli. *Who'd A Thought It: Improvisation in African-American Quiltmaking*. San Francisco: San Francisco Craft and Folk Art Museum, 1987.

Lipsett, Linda Otto. *Remember Me: Women and Their Friendship Quilts*. San Francisco: Quilt Digest Press, 1985.

Mathieson, Judy. *Mariner's Compass: An American Quilt Classic*. Lafayette, CA: C & T Publishing, 1987.

Mathieson, Judy. "Some Sources of Design Inspiration for the Quilt Pattern Mariner's Compass." In *Uncoverings 1981*. Mill Valley, CA: The American Quilt Study Group, 1982

McCloskey, Marsha. *Feathered Star Quilts*. Bothell, WA: That Patchwork Place, Inc., 1987.

McLaurin, Melton and Thomason, Michael. *Mobile: The Life and Times of a Great Southern City*. Woodland Hills, CA: Windsor Publications, 1981.

McMorris, Penny. *Crazy Quilts*. New York: E. P. Dutton, 1984.

Montgomery, Florence M. *Printed Textiles: English and American Cottons and Linens: 1700–1850*. New York: The Viking Press, A Winterthur Book, 1970.

Montgomery, Florence M. *Textiles in America: 1650–1870*. New York: W.W. Norton & Company, 1984.

Nelson, Cyril I. and Houck, Carter. *The Quilt Engagement Calendar Treasury.* New York: E. P. Dutton, Inc., 1982.

The Oakland Museum History Department. *American Quilts: A Handmade Legacy,* edited by Thomas L. Frye. Oakland, CA: The Oakland Museum, 1981.

Orlofsky, Patsy and Myron. *Quilts in America.* New York: McGraw-Hill Book Company, 1974.

Pellman, Rachel and Pellman, Kenneth. *The World of Amish Quilts.* Intercourse, PA: Good Books, 1984.

Quilt National. *The Quilt: New Directions for an American Tradition.* Exton, PA: Schiffer Publishing Limited, 1983.

Ramsey, Bets and Waldvogel, Merikay. *The Quilts of Tennessee.* Nashville: Rutledge Hill Press, 1986.

Ramsey, Bets. *Old and New Quilt Patterns in the Southern Tradition.* Nashville: Rutledge Hill Press, 1987.

Rehmel, Judy. *The Quilt I.D. Book.* New York: Prentice Hall Press, 1986.

Roberson, Ruth, ed. *North Carolina Quilts.* Chapel Hill: The University of North Carolina Press, 1988.

Robertson, Elizabeth Wells. *American Quilts.* New York: The Studio Publications, Inc., 1948.

Safford, Carleton L. and Bishop, Robert. *America's Quilts and Coverlets.* New York: Barre Publishing Company, Inc., Weathervane Books, 1974.

Swann, Susan Burrows. *Plain & Fancy: American Women and Their Needlework, 1700–1850.* New York: Holt, Rinehart & Winston, A Rutledge Book, 1977.

Texas Heritage Quilt Society. *Texas Quilts, Texas Treasures.* Paducah, KY: American Quilter's Society, 1986.

Trechsel, Gail Andrews and MacDonald, Janet Strain. *Black Belt to Hill Country: Alabama Quilts from the Robert and Helen Cargo Collection* (catalog from the Birmingham Museum of Art exhibition of the same name; no publication data given) c. 1982.

Woodard, Thomas K. and Greenstein, Blanche. *Twentieth Century Quilts: 1900–1950.* New York: E. P. Dutton, 1988.

Webster, Marie. *Quilts: Their Story and How to Make Them.* Garden City, NY: Doubleday, Doran & Company, 1928.

NOTES

1. Rachel Pellman and Kenneth Pellman, *The World of Amish Quilts* (Intercourse, PA: Good Books, 1984), 52.

2. Gail Binney, *Homage to Amanda* (San Francisco: RK Press, 1984), 36.

3. Barbara Brackman, *Clues in the Calico* (McLean, VA: EPM Publications, Inc., 1989), 171.

4. Texas Heritage Quilt Society, *Texas Quilts, Texas Treasures* (Paducah, KY: American Quilter's Society, 1986), 37.

5. The Kentucky Quilt Project, *Kentucky Quilts, 1800–1900* (Louisville, KY: Time Capsules: The Kentucky Quilt Project, 1982), 23.

6. John Rice Irwin, *A People and Their Quilts* (Exton, PA: Schiffer Publishing Ltd, 1984), 133.

7. Gail Andrews Trechsel and Janet Strain MacDonald, *Black Belt to Hill Country: Alabama Quilts from the Robert and Helen Cargo Collection* (catalog from the Birmingham Museum of Art exhibition of the same name; no publication data given; c. 1982), 64–65.

8. Carol LaBranche, *A Constellation for Quilters; Star Patterns for Piecing* (Pittstown, NJ: The Main Street Press, 1986), 21.

9. The Kentucky Quilt Project, *Kentucky Quilts, 1800–1900* (Louisville, KY: Time Capsules: The Kentucky Quilt Project, 1982), 57.

10. Judy Mathieson, "Some Published Sources of Design Inspiration for the Quilt Pattern Mariner's Compass— 17th to 20th Century," *Uncoverings 1981* (Mill Valley, CA: The American Quilt Study Group, 1982), 12.

11. Ibid., 14.

12. Barbara Brackman, *An Encyclopedia of Pieced Quilt Patterns, Volume 8* (Lawrence, KS: Prairie Flower Publishing, 1983), 528.

13. Ibid.

14. Marsha McClosky, *Feathered Star Quilts* (Bothell, WA: That Patchwork Place, 1987), 34.

15. Florence Montgomery, *Printed Textiles: English and American Cottons and Linens, 1700–1800* (New York: The Viking Press, A Winterthur Book, 1970), 306.

INDEX